EVERY MAN'S BOOK OF SAINTS

Following the ASB Calendar

C. P. S. Clarke's original text
revised and supplemented by

Brother Kenneth, CGA

MOWBRAY
LONDON & OXFORD

ISBN 0 264 66556 2 paperback

First published 1981
by A. R. Mowbray & Co. Ltd.
Saint Thomas House, Becket Street
Oxford, OX1 1SJ

Typeset in 'Monophoto' Bembo by
Cotswold Typesetting Ltd., Gloucester.
Printed in Great Britain by
The Thetford Press Ltd., Thetford, Norfolk.

Preface

For some of us, the new Calendar of *The Alternative Service Book 1980* is a source of quiet satisfaction. For years we have desired to see such people as Nicholas Ferrar, Launcelot Andrewes, William Wilberforce commemorated in the Calendar of the Church, which is the richer for numbering them among her sons. Of course there are names that do appear which one might want to see left out; there are names too that do not find a place there, but no matter. The Calendar has been revised and for that give thanks.

However it would be idle to suppose that all members of our congregations are familiar with the lives of those who are recalled annually in our worship. This revision of a previous revision of Archdeacon Clarke's *Everyman's Book of Saints* has been designed so that before a service, or perhaps within it, it will be possible without a great deal of research to read out something about the saint who is to be commemorated. Some of the stories are far too long for that, even, and where the life of a saint has taken up more than a single paragraph, a paragraph summary of the life will appear at the end of the entry.

The saints appear in calendrical order, and if the reader happens to consult the index and realises that there are many more names than actual entries, that is because nearly all the saints mentioned in the text appear in the index to help anyone who uses the volume as a reference book.

*　　*　　*

Finally I record my deep gratitude to Mrs Connie Tyrell and Mr Jim Scott for typing the revised manuscript. Without their loving help the work would never have been completed.

William Law's Day, 1981   KENNETH, CGA

St Hilary 13 JANUARY

Bishop of Poitiers, Teacher of the Faith, 367

Hilary, born at Poitiers in the fourth century, was of pagan aristocracy and not converted to Christianity until he reached manhood. In spite of his reluctance to accept the bishopric of Poitiers, it was almost forced upon him, and the qualities which had made him eminent in Gaul became apparent to the whole Church. After his refusal to sign the condemnation of St Athanasius the Emperor Constantius banished Hilary to Phrygia. His exile lasted for three years, during which time he wrote several treatises, the best known being *On the Trinity*. His uncompromising and effective opposition to the Arians was such that Constantius was obliged to restore him to Gaul in order that the saint might not disturb the Arian influence in the East. In 304 Hilary journeyed to Milan, where in public debate he led the Arian Bishop Auxentius to confess Christ as being of one substance with the Father. He died at Poitiers around the year 367.

St Antony of Egypt   17 JANUARY
Abbot, 356

St Antony of Egypt is one of the band of wealthy men who have taken our Lord's command to the rich young man to sell all that he had and give to the poor, quite literally. When he had rid himself of all his possessions, and placed his younger sister, hopefully with her consent, in a convent, he began to live as a hermit.

St Antony put himself under the instruction of experienced solitaries of holy life, learning something from each. St Athanasius says 'he contemplated the courtesy of one, and another's assiduity in prayer; another's freedom from anger; another's love of mankind'. And so he trained himself, working with his hands, imposing increasing austerities on himself and praying continually. In spite of his ascetic life he was constantly tempted by impurity, by doubts of his vocation, and by a young man's natural love of pleasure and human affections. The devil appeared to him in visible form as a beautiful woman and as a black child, and finally, unable to overthrow him, the evil one fell down before him crying 'I have deceived many, I have cast down many, but now I have been worsted in the battle'.

Antony was still subject to continual temptation, and he sought greater solitude in an ancient tomb. Here he was assailed by demons who beat him until he was unable to stand. He challenged them: 'If you can and have received power against me, don't delay; but if you cannot, why do you disturb me in vain? For a seal to us and wall of safety is our faith in the Lord'. At these words the roof of the tomb opened and a ray of light fell upon Antony. The demons vanished and his pain ceased.

For almost twenty years he lived in some ruins on a mountain, seeing no one except a man who brought him bread twice a year. At the age of fifty-four he came down from the mountain to found his first monastery which may have been a collection of cells inhabited by solitary ascetics living under rule. This is commonly thought to have been the beginning of Christian monasticism.

In the year 311 St Antony left his cell to go to Alexandria

where the Church was being persecuted by Maximus. There he openly encouraged and defended the martyrs, but although he would have preferred to share their heroic fate he thought it presumptuous to provoke martyrdom deliberately. At the end of the persecution he returned to his monastery. Later he founded another at Pispir, but for the most part he chose to continue in his solitary life. He made a little garden on his mountain top and spent his days between prayer and manual work, sometimes making mats of palm leaves and praying as he wove. He taught his monks that perfection existed in the love of God rather than in mortification.

St Antony visited Alexandria once more in order to confute the Arian heresy, of which he had a particular horror. He made many converts and worked miracles. When the Governor desired him to stay longer he answered, 'As fish die when they are taken from the water, so does a monk wither away if he forsake his solitude'.

Shortly before his death St Antony visited his monks for the last time. In spite of their entreaties that he should stay with them till the end, he returned to his cell on Mount Kolzim near the Red Sea. He ordered his disciples, Macarius and Amathas to bury his body secretly in that place. 'Farewell, my children, Antony is departing and will no longer be with you'. With these words the founder of monasticism, and the greatest of hermits stretched himself out and, without any other sign, calmly ceased to breathe.

SHORT VERSION (*St Antony of Egypt*)
St Antony of Egypt is often considered the founder of Christian monasticism. He was a rich Egyptian who gave away all his possessions and began to live as a hermit. Artists usually depict him in his solitary fights against demons, and one of the stories told about him concerns Satan who appeared to him in the guise of a beautiful woman, but failed to tear Antony away from his Lord. When he was fifty-four he founded his first group of hermits living according to a common rule, but in 311 he left his cell for a while to go to Alexandria to encourage the Christians there undergoing persecution. He was to return once more to Alexandria to confute the Arians, but despite the

Governor's plea, he returned to his mountain, to spend his days in prayer, working his garden or sometimes making mats of palm leaves. He was 105 when he died on Mount Kolzim near the Red Sea in AD 356.

St Agnes

Virgin, Martyr, 304

At the time of her death Agnes was thirteen, and had already rejected many suitors including the son of the Prefect of Rome on the grounds that she had consecrated her virginity to our Lord. She was denounced to the governor as a Christian, but the judge urged her to consider her position for she was only a child. She replied, 'I may be a child, but faith dwells not in years but in the heart'. Agnes was then faced with a display of instruments of torture, but she remained fearless and undismayed. Unable to shake her resolution the judge condemned her to be thrown into a brothel, but the profligates who had followed her into the house of ill fame were so awed by the saint that none dared approach her. The governor, enraged by her refusal to be intimidated, threatened to burn her alive, but even at the stake she prayed, 'I bless you, Father of my Lord Jesus Christ'. At her words the flames died down, and still refusing to recant, Agnes was despatched with a sword.

St Francis de Sales   24 JANUARY
Bishop, Teacher of the Faith, 1622

Francis de Sales is one of the many saints within the Catholic/Protestant divide who was quite convinced that if men and women died outside the Catholic Church, by which he meant, among other things, acknowledging the authority of the Pope, they were damned. Protestants held similar views about those misguided enough to die as Catholics. It is for his holiness and his spiritual vision that all Christians may gratefully commemorate Francis in these more ecumenical days.

He was ordained in Geneva and spent his whole ministry in that diocese, first as a missioner in company with his cousin, Canon Louis de Sales, in the Chablais which at that time was a Calvinist stronghold. When he arrived there, having set out on foot in September, 1594, the people of the district were getting used to the idea that they had recently become subjects of the Duke of Savoy, who was a Catholic. Years later, writing to the Pope, St Francis described the desolation which greeted them in the Chablais: ' . . . nothing but heart breaking sights met our eyes. Out of sixty-five parishes, excepting for a few officers of the Duke's garrisons, there were scarcely fifty Catholics. The churches were desecrated or destroyed, and the cross everywhere broken down'.

They met with every kind of opposition. For the sake of safety the cousins were quartered in the Chateau des Allinges, six or seven miles from Thonon, the capital town, since the governor of the province was stationed at Allinges with a garrison. They preached daily in Thonon and gradually spread their message farther and farther afield. Their daily journeys exposed them to considerable danger; fanatical Calvinists had sworn to kill them and made several attempts to do so. On one occasion Francis was benighted in a snow-bound wood and was obliged to spend the night in a tree to escape wolves. He wrote to a friend: 'We are but making a beginning. I shall go on in good courage, and I hope in God against all human hope'.

The saint began to write leaflets answering the principal objections to the faith. These were copied by hand and distributed in various ways, and gradually they began to take effect. They were later to form the volume of *Controversies* and were the beginning of his work as a writer. Apart from his sermons and pamphlets, the perseverance of St Francis, his courage, endurance and gentleness spoke forcibly to the peasants of the Chablais, conversions became frequent, and lapsed Catholics sought reconciliation with their Church in ever increasing numbers. After three or four years it was possible for the visiting Bishop de Granier to administer confirmation. In the September of that same year the Chablais ceased officially to be Protestant. The few remaining heretics were ordered by the Duke of Savoy to cross the lake into the land of Vaud, just as they had expelled the Catholics.

In 1599, St Francis was appointed coadjutor Bishop of Geneva. He went to Rome for a theological examination and his appointment was confirmed. In 1602 he went to Paris and preached a course of sermons in the chapel royal. Henry IV offered him every inducement to remain in Paris, but Francis replied that he had married a poor bride and could not forsake her for a richer.

At the death of Bishop de Granier, Francis succeeded to the see of Geneva in 1602. His establishment at Annecy was run on lines of severe economy, and he gave away his private fortune, saying: 'When one has but little, one has little to give, little to answer for. No one is really poor who has enough to live on. Had it been the will of God I would rather have been a humble priest, carrying holy water and tending a few poor people, than wear the mitre and staff.

In his own life he practised severe mortifications, but he never allowed asceticism to get the better of common sense. 'God would have us treat our bodies according to their capacity; we must deal patiently and charitably with them as poor infirm creatures. The spirit cannot get on with an overfed body, but if the body is underfed it cannot get on with the spirit. We must treat the body like a child, correct it duly but not overwhelm it.'

He governed the diocese by love and gentleness, and some held it against him that he showed excessive indulgence to heretics. He ruled that it was better to make penitents by gentleness than hypocrites by severity, but he could be stern when gentleness could not prevail. When a cleric spoke of his unworthiness for his office, he replied, 'Yes, I am quite aware of it, and perhaps I see it even more plainly than you do'. But he followed the snub with useful advice and encouragement.

St Francis instituted a children's catechising on Sunday afternoons at the cathedral, which he generally took himself. Before service a choirboy was sent round the town of Annecy ringing a bell and calling out: 'Come and learn the way to Paradise by means of Christian doctrine'. When someone complained of the troops of children who followed him about, he replied: 'Suffer them to come, they are my own dear little people'. He arranged for the poorest and most repulsive people to come to him for their confessions.

He founded the Order of the Visitation with St Jane Frances de Chantal. At first the members took no vows but occupied themselves with the care of the sick. Later, greatly against his wish, they became enclosed, subject to the usual vows.

In spite of his incessant work in his diocese, Francis published his book, *Introduction to the Devout Life*, which has become one of the great classics of devotion. It was written from scattered notes of instruction and advice which he wrote to Madame de Charmoisy, a Parisian penitent who had placed herself under his guidance. In 1616 he published his *Treatise on the Love of God*, in which he wrote that 'the measure of love, is to love without measure'.

He visited Paris again in 1618 and stayed there a year. He was offered, and refused, the office of coadjutor Bishop of Paris with the right of succession. 'One does not give oneself to the Church in order to secure a position, but to till that piece of ground allotted by the householder.'

After an exhausting journey to Avignon to meet Louis XIII and the Duke of Savoy, St Francis de Sales was taken ill with a paralytic seizure at Lyons on the return journey. He died on 28 December, 1622, worn out with a life of toil.

SHORT VERSION (*St Francis de Sales*)
St Francis de Sales was ordained in the Diocese of Geneva in 1593. When he died in 1622 he had served the people of God there, first as priest of the Chablais where he was largely responsible for the conversion of many Calvinists to the

Catholic way of looking at things; next as coadjutor Bishop, and finally as Bishop. His private money he gave away, and lived very simply, resisting all efforts of the French king to get him to move to Paris. He governed his diocese by love and gentleness. Children adored him and he himself taught those who came to his cathedral for instruction. Francis was responsible for that great classic about the life of the spirit, *Introduction to the Devout Life*, based on notes which he originally wrote for one of his penitents. He died of a stroke at Lyons when he was fifty-five.

St Paul

Apostle and Martyr, c.67

St Paul, Saul is the Hebrew version of his name, was born at Tarsus and enjoyed the privileges of Roman citizenship. By birth he was a Jew of the tribe of Benjamin. He learnt the trade of tentmaker but his parents also sent him to Jerusalem to study under Gamaliel, a distinguished scholar and a Pharisee. Saul accepted the philosophy of the Pharisees with enthusiasm since it appeared to him to be the final revelation of the divine will. This made it natural that he should later make havoc of the Church with all the ardour of which he was capable.

Saul assisted passively in the murder of St Stephen by holding the garments of those who were stoning the saint. Later he applied for a commission to arrest all the Jews of Damascus who confessed Christ, and to bring them as prisoners to Jerusalem. The story of what befell can only be told in the words of the New Testament: 'While he was still on the road and nearing Damascus, suddenly a light flashed from the sky all around him. He fell to the ground and heard a voice saying "Saul, Saul, why do you persecute me?" "Tell me Lord," he said, "who are you". The voice answered, "I am Jesus, whom you are persecuting". 'And he, trembling and astonished, said "Lord what do you want me to do?"' Those who travelled with Saul heard the voice, but saw nothing, and when Saul rose from the ground he was blind and they led him by the hand to Damascus. There Saul remained for three days, fasting and sightless, until a disciple called Ananias came to him at the Lord's bidding and, laying hands on him, restored his sight. Saul was baptised and, throwing in his lot with the disciples, began to preach Christianity in the synagogues. The Jews of Damascus, perceiving a serious threat in this powerful apostate from the orthodox faith, plotted to kill Saul and he was obliged to flee to Jerusalem.

At Jerusalem he was naturally regarded with suspicion by the Christians, but Barnabas assured them of his good faith, and he began to preach openly and enter into debate with the Greeks. But again his life was known to be in danger and the brethren sent him to Tarsus. For some time there was a pause in the persecution, the churches increased and Saul seems to have remained in Tarsus for seven or eight years.

In the year 44 St Barnabas, who had been sent to minister to the Gentile Christians in Antioch, came to Tarsus and fetched him to help in the work. In the following year they started on their first missionary journey; the great work of Paul's life was begun. In his missionary labours he showed himself to be an inspired strategist, a diplomatist, and a strict disciplinarian, as well as a saint. His plan was to make use of the Roman imperial administration, by establishing the Church strongly in the centres of the different provinces he was able to reach, that from them the gospel might spread to the smaller towns and villages.

Pisidian Antioch, the centre of the southern part of the province of Galatia, was the first to be thus occupied. It was followed by the foundation of the Church in Thessalonica and Philippi in Macedonia, at Corinth in Achaia, and at Ephesus in Asia, and having accomplished this he saw that he must do the same at Rome itself.

If the conception showed a man of genius its realisation demanded courage, determination, energy and entire self-devotion. He had to contend with great physical difficulties that tried the body, quite apart from the recurrent illness of which he speaks as his 'thorn in the flesh'; he worked hard, constantly in danger, 'weary and in pain, hungry, thirsty, cold and naked'. He had to face the opposition of the heathen, and of the Jews, who were even more bitterly opposed. Worst of all were 'the perils among false brethren', those who while accepting Christ wished to keep the Jewish law and force its acceptance on the Gentiles who joined the Church. St Paul had not only to convert the heathen; he had also to secure for them a place in the Church, which was no easy matter. Even after the Council at Jerusalem had pronounced in his favour, some Jewish Christians came to Antioch and disturbed the Church there, even bringing St Peter to their side, so that St Paul had to rebuke him publicly. He was pursued by the hostility of these Judaisers even in captivity in Rome, and his letters to the Galatians and Romans were written principally to confute their errors.

He unfolded his record to the Corinthians. 'I have been sent to prison more often, and whipped so many times more, often almost to death. Five times I had the thirty-nine lashes from the Jews, three times I have been beaten with sticks, once I was stoned.'

His Roman citizenship secured him a safe passage to Caesarea and fair trial before King Agrippa when the Jews would have torn him to pieces in Jerusalem after his appearance in the temple. In Rome he was imprisoned for two years in a private house which he hired. His only guard was a single soldier to whom he was chained. There he wrote some of his letters 'and welcomed all who came to see him preaching the kingdom of God, and teaching concerning the Lord Jesus Christ, with complete freedom and without hindrance'. He was, however, acquitted and released about the year 62.

There is no record in the New Testament of how the next few years were spent. But it seems certain that he revisited the churches he had founded in the East, and at least highly probable that he fulfilled his intention of preaching in Spain. There is no foundation for the legend that he preached in Britain. Tradition has it that he was imprisoned a second time in Rome, and beheaded probably in AD 67.

St Timothy and
St Titus

Timothy was born at Lystra of mixed parentage, his mother being a Jewess and his father a Gentile. He accompanied Paul on his second missionary journey, and was frequently entrusted by Paul with visits on behalf of the apostle to the young churches at Thessalonica and Corinth. He remained with Paul during his first imprisonment in Rome and was sent from there to Ephesus where he is said to have become its first Bishop. There he continued opposition to the cult of the goddess Diana, and was killed by her supporters AD 97.

Titus was another of Paul's companions, and was with the apostle as he returned for the Council of Jerusalem after the first missionary journey. Paul sent him as his representative to the church at Corinth and left him behind at Crete to lead the new church there. Titus is believed to have become the first Bishop of the church in Crete and to have been buried at Gortyna, the ancient capital of the island.

St John Chrysostom 27 JANUARY
Bishop of Constantinople, Teacher of the Faith, 407

St John, surnamed Chrysostom, or Golden Mouth, on account of his eloquence, was born at Antioch about the year 347, and as a lad sent to study under Libanius, the foremost orator of his day. John attained such proficiency in the art that when Libanius was asked on his deathbed which of his pupils should succeed him, replied, 'John would have been my choice, had not the Christians stolen him from us'.

At some time in early manhood St John decided against practising law, which appeared to him inconsistent with the practice of Christianity. His decision seems to have coincided with his baptism, which took place when he was about twenty-three. Together with his friend Basil, also to be canonised, he entered a religious community in the mountains south of Antioch. He passed four years with the community, and two in a cave as a solitary. His health broke down and he was obliged to return to Antioch. He was ordained deacon by St Meletius in 381, and in 386 he was ordained priest by Bishop Flavian, who appointed him as his preacher.

For twelve years Chrysostom continued as the bishop's deputy, his duties increasing as Flavian declined into old age. He looked upon the instruction and care of the poor as his first responsibility, and he preached to congregations so large and so absorbed by his sermons that he was obliged to warn them to leave their purses at home because of the number of pickpockets who found them an easy prey.

When the citizens of Antioch went on the rampage destroying the statues of the imperial family after the imposition of a new tax, their Bishop had to plead with the Emperor for clemency toward his flock, and John's famous 'Sermon on the Statues' preached at the time, converted many and established him as one of the great spiritual forces of the Eastern Empire.

In the year 397 Chrysostom left Antioch at the invitation of an officer of the Emperor Arcadius in order to visit the tombs of the martyrs outside the city. There he was seized and carried off to Constantinople where he was consecrated Archbishop.

Arcadius had devised the stratagem, and once St. John found himself at Constantinople he submitted to the inevitable.

He set about a programme of reform, beginning with his own household. Cutting down his expenses he gave his savings to the poor and to the support of hospitals. His autocratic methods brought him into collision with his clergy, the wealthy lay Christians, and finally with the Empress Eudoxia. In his tactlessness he showed an insensitivity curious in one who was able to convert innumerable sinners, pagans and heretics. To these he cried, 'If you have fallen a second time, or even a thousand times into sin, come to me, and you shall be healed'. They came to him, and were healed, but to the impenitent he was merciless.

As a result of intrigue between his enemies however, John was tried and finally banished from Constantinople. Travelling from Nicaea to Cucusus in Armenia he suffered great hardships. He was kindly received by the Bishop of Cucusus and it was from there that he sent to St Olympias his famous treatise on the theme 'That no one can hurt him who does not hurt himself'.

But he was not to rest at Cucusus. His enemies secured an order that he was to be taken to Pityus. He was ill-treated on the journey and died of exhaustion at the Chapel of St Basilicus in the year AD 407.

SHORT VERSION (*St John Chrysostom*)
His second name Chrysostom is Greek for 'golden mouthed' and as a young man he trained to be a lawyer, but he decided against it and became a monk instead. However, he was not fit enough and so returned home to Antioch, where he was ordained and became preacher to his bishop and frequently acted as his deputy. His fame spread and in 397 by the stratagems of the Emperor, John Chrysostom was kidnapped, taken to Constantinople and consecrated its Bishop. There his straight speaking and also his tactlessness eventually won him the enmity of the Empress. He was banished from the city and died on his journey into exile in 407.

St Thomas Aquinas

Priest, Teacher of the Faith, 1274

St Thomas has been described as the most learned of the saints and the most saintly of the learned. He was born near Aquino, in Italy of a distinguished family, descended from the Lombards. He was educated first at the Benedictine monastery of Monte Cassino, and at thirteen he entered the University of Naples where he studied the arts and sciences. It was at Naples the he began to frequent the Church of the Dominicans and at nineteen he was received into the order, without the consent of his family. His parents had wanted him to become a Benedictine, and when they learned that he had joined the Order of Preachers his mother pursued him from Naples to Rome in an attempt to persuade him to change his mind. When Theodora arrived in Rome her son was already on his way to Bologna, but his brothers waylaid him and took him by force to his home, and thence to a castle two miles distant where he was imprisoned for two years.

In spite of threats and deliberate temptations, Thomas's resolution held, and in 1245 his family resigned themselves to the inevitable and he was allowed to return to his order. During his imprisonment he had continued to study, and is thought to have written a treatise on the fallacies of Aristotle.

Thomas was sent to complete his studies under Albertus Magnus at Cologne. He was silent, humble and pious. For some time his abilities were not apparent and he was nicknamed 'the dumb Sicilian ox'. One day he was given a public test at which he acquitted himself so brilliantly, that his master exclaimed: 'We call Brother Thomas "the dumb ox"; but I tell you that he will yet make his lowing heard to the uttermost parts of the earth'.

Thomas was appointed second professor at the Dominican school in Cologne and in 1252 was sent to Paris. He then returned to Italy for nine years as preacher general, and taught in a school of scholars attached to the papal court. In 1269 he left for Paris where the King, St Louis IX, often consulted him on important matters of state.

Thomas was then engaged on the most famous of his

writings, the *Summa Theologica*. Once, while at lunch with St Louis, he emerged from a profound reverie to strike the table with his fist and exclaim loudly, 'That's finished the Manichean heresy!'. Reminded that he was at table with the King, he recovered himself and apologised for his absence of mind. He was recalled to Italy in 1272. While celebrating Mass on the feast of St Nicholas, he saw a vision which affected him so deeply that from that time he wrote no more. His *Summa Theologica*, an exposition of the Christian religion, was never finished. Urged to complete it, he replied: 'The end of my labours is come. All that I have written appears to be as so much straw after the things that have been revealed to me'. He was already ill when he set out to attend the General Council at Lyons. On the journey he became worse and he died on 7th March 1274.

SHORT VERSION (*St Thomas Aquinas*)
St Thomas Aquinas, the Angelic Doctor, most learned of the saints and the most saintly of the learned, despite his parents' opposition, joined St Dominic's Order of Preachers when he was nineteen. At his studies in Cologne he was nicknamed 'the dumb Sicilian ox' but his intellectual genius eventually revealed itself and in 1252 he began his career as a university lecturer. Seventeen years later he was sent by his order to Paris where he taught at its university and became the confidant of the King, St Louis IX. It was there that he began his famous theological exposition of Christianity, *Summa Theologica*, which though very long was never finished. When his brothers urged him to complete it he replied: 'The end of my labours is come. All that I have written appears to be as so much straw after the things that have been revealed to me'. He died in 1274.

Charles I

King, Martyr, 1649

A modern historian suggested that if, by his life, King Charles nearly destroyed the monarchy in England, he saved it by his death. That may or may not be true, but it is certain that Charles eventually went to his death because although he was prepared to compromise in many areas of his royal prerogative, he was not prepared to see the Church of England lose its bishops, and become presbyterian, though he even went as far as agreeing to bishops in presbytery. After the restoration of his son Charles II, the Convocation of the Church declared his father King Charles the Martyr and several churches were built in his honour.

In his private life he was an affectionate father and a faithful and loving husband, virtues not common among kings. 'He was sober in the wildest youth, when all others are loose and wild; he was humble in the glories of a court, which usually makes others giddy and vain.' He was devout and punctilious in the performance of his religious duties. 'Even when he went hunting he never failed before he sat down to dinner to hear part of the Liturgy read to him.' At Newcastle he spent two hours daily in private prayer, besides saying Matins and Evensong. No English sovereign ever lived his life more wholeheartedly in the sight and fear of God and with a more single eye to his glory.

'When the state of his soul required he was as ready to perform those more severe parts of religion which seem most distasteful to flesh and blood. And he never refused to take to himself the shame of those acts wherein he had transgressed, that he might give glory to his God. For after the army had forced him from Holmeby, and in their several removes had brought him to Latmas, an house of the Earl of Devonshire, on August 1st being Sunday, in the morning, before Sermon, he led forth with him into the garden the Rev. Dr Sheldon (who attended on him, and whom he was pleased to use as his confessor), and drawing out of his pocket a paper commanded him to read it, transcribe it, and so deliver it to him again. This paper contained several vows which he had obliged his soul unto for the glory of his Maker, the advance of true piety, and the emolument of the Church. And among them was this one, that he would do public penance for the injustice he had suffered to be done to the Earl of Strafford; and adjured the Doctor that if he ever saw him in a condition to observe that or any other of those vows he should solicitously mind him of the obligations, as he dreaded the guilt of the breach should lie upon his own soul.'

The upshot of what Lord Clarendon calls 'The Great Rebellion' but most history books refer to as the Civil War was that Charles was brought to trial by Parliament. Naturally the King refused to recognise the court's authority but he was nevertheless sentenced to death. The next evening when Bishop Juxon of London came to condole with him, Charles replied: 'Leave off this, my lord; we have not time for it. Let us think of our great work, and prepare to meet that great God to whom, ere long, I am to give an account of myself. We will not talk of these rogues in whose hands I am; they thirst after my blood and they will have it . . . and God's will be done. I thank God I heartily forgive them, and I will talk of them no more.' On the morning of 30 January 1649 he rose at four, and, after spending an hour in prayer, called to be dressed, and insisted on having his toilet performed with as much care as usual. 'I am to be espoused to my blessed Jesus today, and must be trim,' he explained. It was a cold morning and so he wore two shirts, lest if his enemies saw him shivering they might think he was afraid. He was led to Whitehall and after a cruel delay of over four hours, came out of the banqueting house to the scaffold where he was beheaded. He was buried at St George's Chapel, Windsor, by Juxon; but permission to use the Prayer Book service at his funeral was refused.

SHORT VERSION (*Charles I*)
It is certain that had he been prepared to surrender bishops within the Church of England, King Charles could have saved his life. He was a very faithful and devoted son of the English Church, and when his opponents looked into his private life the worst they could bring against him was that he read Shakespeare! In 1649 the Parliamentarians tried him in the

Great Hall at Westminster, but naturally he refused to recognise the authority of the court. Nevertheless he was sentenced to death and the nobility of his death on 30 January 1649 moved even his enemies.

Saints and Martyrs of Europe

This commemoration might include:

St Blasius, *Bishop, Martyr, c.316*

This day is also his feast day. He is one of many, many, early European Saints about whom we know little apart from their names. Blasius is said to have been Bishop of Sebaste, and died a martyr's death by being flogged with iron-wool combs.

St Sergius, *Abbot, 1392*

He was born at Rostov and when he was twenty-one he founded a monastary near Radonezh, north-east of Moscow. Sergius' shining love of God and his fellow men, drew all kinds of people to seek his advice, including Prince Dimitri. It was this prince, encouraged by Sergius, who defeated the Tartar invaders, while Sergius and his monks were praying for those killed in the decisive battle. Sergius, the great national Russian Saint, died in his Holy Trinity Monastery in 1392. His own feast day is 25 September.

St Ignatius Loyola, *Priest, Founder of the Society of Jesus, 1556*

Ignatius, the founder of the Jesuits was a Spaniard brought up to be a soldier. As a result of a wound he was confined to bed and there read a life of the Saviour which so moved him that Ignatius decided to become Christ's soldier and to seek companions to serve as soldiers with him. His community was the spearhead of much missionary endeavour throughout the world; though Ignatius lived much of his life in Rome directing the affairs of his order, seeing it grow to a thousand men before he died suddenly on 31 July 1556.

Twentieth century European saints include: SS John of Kronstadt, Nectarios of Pentapolis, Gemma Galgani, Pius X, Maria Goretti, Bertilla Boscardin, Rafaela Maria Porras, Blessed Maximilian Kolbe, Maria Ledochowska, Contardo Ferrini, Giuseppe Toniolo, Giuseppe Moscati, and Charles de Foucauld, Dietrich Bonhoeffer, Matt Talbot.

Saints and Martyrs of Africa

This commemoration might include:

Uganda Martyrs, *1886, 1977*

Mwanga the ruler of Uganda wanted boys for his bed and when Christian pages began to refuse his advances he had all of them, and that included both Catholics and Protestants, put to death. On their way to the place of execution these young Christians sang hymns in honour of our Lord and some were still singing as the flames hissed around them. All this happened in 1886 but in 1977 the Anglican Archbishop Janani Luwum was but one of many Christians, again both Catholics and Protestants, who suffered death under the regime of another tyrant.

Cecile Isherwood, *Religious, 1906*

Cecile was born in England but went to South Africa to work in the diocese of Grahamstown in 1883. At the request of the Bishop she founded a Community of Sisters, to work in the Church of the Province of South Africa, which she led until her death at the early age of forty-four.

Andrew Kaguru and the Martyrs of Kenya, *1953*

During the Mau Mau disturbances a few years before Kenya achieved independence, over one hundred Christians were killed by the Mau Mau, generally because they had refused to take a pagan oath which would bind them to support the attacks on the white farms in the country. Andrew was a catechist at Kiruri and he had been particularly outspoken on the activities of the Mau Mau. As a result he was cut to death because he would not subscribe to the oath.

Other African Saints and Martyrs of the nineteenth and twentieth centuries include: Bernard Mizeke, Thomas Walter Bako, Mary Slessor, Manche Masemula, Yona Kanamuzeyi, Leonard Kamungu, William Percival Johnson, Frank Weston.

St Polycarp

Bishop of Smyrna, Martyr, c.155

St Polycarp was one of a group of early bishops who were the immediate disciples of the apostles. St John consecrated him Bishop of Smyrna in the year 96. He remained its bishop for fifty-nine years and during that time he was to meet Ignatius on his way to Rome and kiss the martyr's chains as he received from Ignatius the Christian flock at Antioch to look after as well. In the sixth year of the reign of the Emperor Marcus Aurelius, persecution broke out in Asia and Polycarp, then an old man, calmly awaited his arrest. He was urged by the proconsul to give up his faith. Polycarp replied: 'Eighty-six years have I served him and he has done me no wrong. How then can I blaspheme my King and my Saviour?' He was sentenced to be burnt and as he was being bound to the stake he prayed: 'Father of your well-beloved Son Jesus Christ, I bless you that you have thought me worthy to share in the number of the martyrs and in the cup of Christ unto the resurrection to eternal life. Wherefore because of these things I praise you, I bless you, I glorify you, through the eternal High Priest, Jesus Christ your well-beloved Son; through whom be glory to you with him in the Holy Spirit both now and for ever'.

George Herbert

27 FEBRUARY

Priest, Pastor, and Poet, 1633

George Herbert was born, and spent his early years in a castle in Montgomery in Wales. When George was only three years old, his father died and his mother, a great friend of the famous poet John Donne, moved to Oxford, but the boy was sent soon afterwards to Westminster School. At sixteen he went to Trinity College, Cambridge, where he worked hard, and after five years was appointed as the Public Orator who had the task of welcoming in a Latin speech, any famous visitors to the university; and also to acknowledge gifts of books for the university library.

One of the first letters of thanks George had to write was to King James I, and after a few visits to Cambridge the King began to take notice of the charm and great gifts of the young orator. Everyone was confident that like his brother Edward, he would enter the King's service and even become an ambassador. The King did in fact give him an annual allowance, and doubtless his mother waited anxiously for news that her son's career was to be still furthered by his monarch.

Perhaps she also thought of his boyhood ambition to become a priest, and of the two possible futures for her boy, an ambassador or a priest, she really hoped for the latter. He had certainly gone to college with every intention of being ordained, but his success with the King had temporarily turned his mind away from his vocation.

King James died when George was thirty-two and it was at that time that he began seriously to consider what God wanted him to be. He went to stay with a friend in the Kent countryside and on his return announced his intention to seek ordination.

A year later he became very ill. He had never been a very strong person, and had to return to the country. This time he went to stay with some distant relations in Wiltshire. By now he had been made deacon but he hesitated to take the final step of being ordained priest, doubting his own worthiness for such a sacred task. He prayed earnestly for a month and then, as an answer to his prayer, he was asked to become Vicar of

24

Bemerton, a little village near Salisbury. The following September, in Salisbury Cathedral, he was ordained a priest.

He had actually been made vicar of his little parish, some months previously and on the day of his induction when he went into the church, to ring the bell which told the parishioners that their new vicar had arrived, he stayed in the church much longer than the congregation, who were outside, expected. At last one of them peeped in through a window and saw their new priest stretched out in front of the altar, offering himself completely to God.

From that day onwards he laboured among them unceasingly. Every day he said Morning and Evening Prayer in his church and every day many joined him. He always rang the bell just before the service so that those in the fields could stop work for a moment and add their prayers too.

George faithfully visited them in their homes when they were sick, and no-one who was cold or hungry called at his house in vain. His wife shared this part of his work and also looked after her husband's three orphaned nieces. It is, however, for his poems that George Herbert is best remembered. Like everything else that he did, his poetry was written for and about God, and hundreds of people still read and love them.

He always went to Salisbury Cathedral once a week, to hear the choir sing Evensong and he used to say that the music was his heaven on earth. Afterwards he would go to a friend's house and there would play his fiddle or sing with others who enjoyed music and singing as much as he did.

Once they were all waiting for him and were beginning to get anxious because Evensong was over and still he had not arrived. At long last he did come but his clothes were in such a mess they all wondered what could have happened to him. He told them that as he was walking to the city he had met a poor man, with a poorer horse, that had fallen under its heavy load. The man was struggling to help his horse, and so Herbert, without thinking of the music he would miss, stripped off his coat and helped the man to unload his cart, allow the horse to stand up and then reload. Finally he gave the poor man some money so that he might refresh himself and his horse before he continued his journey.

Such was the man the parishioners of Bemerton had for their

priest. He still was not a strong man and at the age of thirty-nine he fell very ill. Knowing that he was dying, he sent the manuscripts of his poems to his friend, Nicholas Ferrar, asking him to publish them only if he thought they would help other Christians to love and serve God. He died on Friday, 1 March 1633 having on the previous Sunday, although in much pain, tuned his fiddle and there sung his own poem in praise of God's day.

SHORT VERSION (*George Herbert*)

Every hymn-book of the English speaking world is likely to contain at least one of George Herbert's poems. As a young man George had hopes for a career in government service, especially when he took the eye of James I on a visit to Cambridge. However at thirty-three his mind turned back to a boyhood desire for ordination. He became Vicar of Bemerton near Salisbury and served the people faithfully as their parish priest for the remaining five years of his life. On his death bed he sent the manuscript of some poems to his friend Nicholas Ferrar with instructions to publish them if he thought they would be of any value for other Christians on their pilgrimage to God. It is a matter for great thanksgiving that they were given thus to us all.

St David

Bishop, Patron Saint of Wales, c.601

In the biography of the saint written by the son of an eleventh century Bishop of St Davids it is difficult to disentangle fact from legend. Legend says that David, born around 520, was the son of Sant, of royal descent, and that his mother was St Non, a grand-daughter of Brychan of Brecknock. After ordination as a priest he studied under the Welsh saint, Paulinus, and is credited with the foundation of twelve monasteries, scattered as far apart as Glastonbury and Leominster. It is also said that he performed many miracles. St David was summoned to the synod which was held at Llandewi Brevi, in Cardiganshire, to suppress the Pelagian heresy, and such was his eloquence and authority the supporters of Pelagianism were silenced. Tradition holds that while David was speaking, a white dove alighted upon his shoulder and the ground rose up under his feet until he was speaking on a hill-top from which his voice sounded like a trumpet to be heard by the thousands gathered in that place. Afterwards David was elected primate of the Welsh Church in succession to St Dubirius, who resigned in his favour, and it was David who moved the episcopal seat from Caerleon to Menevia, the present St Davids, where his community led a life of extreme austerity.

St David died at Menevia, when he was very old. He had been, 'the great ornament and example of his age'. His last words to his flock enjoined them to 'Be joyful, brothers and sisters. Keep your faith, and do the little things that you have seen and heard with me'. 'Kings mourned him as a judge,' wrote Gerald Cambrensis, 'the older people mourned him as a brother, the younger as a father.' 'Who will teach us? Who will help us? Who will pray for us? Who will be a father to us as David was?'

SHORT VERSION (*St David*)

The birth of St David is shrouded in legend, but as a priest he is credited with founding twelve monasteries and was summoned to the synod which was held at Llandewi Brevi, in Cardiganshire, to suppress the Pelagian heresy. Such was his

27

eloquence and authority the supporters of Pelagianism were silenced. Afterwards David was elected primate of the Welsh Church in succession to St Dubirius, who resigned in his favour, and it was David who moved the episcopal seat from Caerleon to Menevia, the present St Davids where his community led a life of extreme austerity. There as an old man David died, mourned by young and old alike.

St Chad

Bishop of Lichfield, Missionary, 672

St Chad was one of four Northumbrian brothers who all became priests, and two, bishops. Chad, with his younger brother Cedd, received his religious training at Lindisfarne under St Aidan. After the death of Aidan, St Chad seems to have spent some years in Ireland with St Egbert, but he returned to England when his brother Cedd summoned him on his death-bed and committed to his charge the abbey of Lastingham, which he himself had founded. But before a year had passed Chad was designated Bishop of York by King Oswy. Later, at the request of Theodore, Archbishop of Canterbury, Chad was appointed Bishop of Mercia.

St Bede writes of him: 'As soon as Chad was consecrated bishop, he began most strenuously to devote himself to ecclesiastical truth and purity of doctrine and to give attention to the practice of humility, self-denial and study: to travel about, not on horseback, but on foot, after the manner of the apostles, preaching the gospel in the towns and the open country, in cottages, villages and castles, for he was one of Aidan's disciples and tried to instruct his hearers by acting and behaving after the example of his master and of his brother Cedd'.

Chad moved the seat of the diocese from Repton to Lichfield, where he built a house of retreat for himself and a few of his monks. A legend exists which attributes the completion of Peterborough minster to him. One day as he prayed by a stream in a wood, a hunted hart leapt into the water. When the huntsmen came up they proved to be the two sons of the apostate King Wulfhere. Chad urged them to show compassion to animals, and converted them to Christianity, but when their father learned that they had renounced paganism he murdered them. Later he repented and, led to St Chad's retreat by the rescued hart, he confessed and did penance. In atonement he built several abbeys and finished the building of Peterborough, which had been commenced by his father. According to the Anglo-Saxon Chronicle, he also contributed to the endowment of Peterborough. St Chad's friend, the monk Owen, relates that one day he heard music descending from heaven to the bishop's oratory, and then ascending again. From his window the Bishop ordered him to call the other monks and when they entered he told them that his death was at hand: 'That gracious guest who was wont to visit our brethren has come to me also today to call me out of this world. Return therefore to the church and speak to the brethren that they pray for my passage to the Lord'. St Chad died seven days later.

SHORT VERSION (*St Chad*)
Chad with his younger brother St Cedd were disciples of St Aidan. When Chad became Bishop of Mercia, 'he began', as St Bede was later to record, 'most strenuously to devote himself to ecclesiastical truth and purity of doctrine and to give attention to the practice of humility, self-denial and study: to travel about, not on horseback, but on foot, after the manner of the apostles, preaching the gospel in the towns and the open country, in cottages, villages and castles, for he was one of Aidan's disciples and tried to instruct his hearers by acting and behaving after the example of his master and of his brother Cedd'. It was Chad who moved the seat of his diocese from Repton to Lichfield, where he built a house of retreat for himself and a few of his monks. He died there in 672.

Ss Perpetua and her Companions
7 MARCH

Carthage, Martyrs, 203

Perpetua, Felicity and their three companions were catechumens arrested in Carthage during the persecution of Severus. The five died in the arena fighting the wild beasts. Perpetua, daughter of a mixed marriage—only her mother was a Christian—wrote a record of their trial and imprisonment, and left it for anyone who watched their martyrdom to complete the story. At a last meal, eaten in public according to custom, the five spoke to those who crowded about them of the judgments of God, and of their joy in their sufferings, and their courage made many converts. Perpetua was twenty-two when she died in the arena.

Edward King
8 MARCH

Bishop of Lincoln, Teacher, Pastor, 1910

Returning from Lincoln Cathedral after Bishop King's funeral someone wrote in a letter, 'We have buried our saint'. He was echoing a little boy in the diocese who many years earlier had asked his mother after a Confirmation service conducted by Edward King, 'Do they always send an angel from heaven to confirm you?' King was consecrated Bishop of Lincoln in 1885 and in that diocese he remained for twenty-five years. He was a devoted pastor, and such was his concern for a chaplain of a prison that he even took over the ministry to a condemned felon, brought the man to repentance, confirmed him and celebrated the Eucharist in the condemned cell just before the execution. In a last letter, dictated before he died, to the people of his diocese he told them, 'My great wish has been to lead you to become Christ-like Christians'. His own example was just like that.

St Patrick   **17 MARCH**

Bishop, Patron Saint of Ireland, c.460

St Patrick was probably of Romano–British extraction, his father being a deacon and a municipal official. Sadly at the age of sixteen, he was carried off by raiders into slavery in pagan Ireland. For six years the young man herded swine, or sheep, most probably in Antrim, or on the coast of Mayo. Homesick he turned to God. In his own words: 'love of God, and his fear, increased more and more, and my faith grew and my spirit was stirred up, so that in a single day I said as many as a hundred prayers and at night nearly as many, so that I used to stay even in the woods and on the mountains. And before the dawn I used to be aroused to prayer, in snow and frost and rain, nor was there any tepidity in me as now I feel, because then the spirit was fervent within me'.

After six years he heard a voice commanding him to escape. Obeying the vision, he travelled two hundred miles to reach the ship which he had been told to join. At first he was refused a passage, but Patrick retired to pray, and shortly afterwards was summoned to take his place in the vessel. They sailed for three days and seem to have landed on the coast of Gaul. There they almost perished from starvation, as the country had been wasted by the Franks. Patrick told them to have faith in his God; he prayed, and almost immediately a herd of swine appeared. The travellers chased and killed all they wanted for themselves and their dogs. Patrick narrates: 'After that they rendered hearty thanks to God, and I became honourable in their eyes; and from that day they had food in abundance.'

Eventually Patrick was restored to his family, who urged him to remain with them, but he was constantly troubled with visions of the pagan Irish imploring him to walk among them once more. The chronological sequence of the events which followed is uncertain, but there is evidence that St Patrick spent many years in France, some on the island of Lerins, in the Mediterranean, and as many as fifteen years in Auxerre, as a pupil of Bishop St Germanus. It seems probable that it was Germanus who consecrated Patrick bishop, and sent him to Britain to replace Palladius, who had died among the Picts less than a year after the beginning of his mission.

32

Patrick was over sixty when he returned to Ireland. Tradition holds that he began his work in Ulster. After that he attempted the conversion of the High-King Laoghaire, whose court was at Tara. It was in Tara that Patrick came into direct conflict with the wizards, or Druids, when he lit the paschal fire at Easter, which happened that year to coincide with the Feast of Tara. It was forbidden to kindle fire before Tara, the penalty of disobedience being death. Patrick's fire lit up the whole of Mag Breg, and the wizards foretold that unless it were quenched the same night it would burn till Doomsday. The King set out with chariots to kill Patrick, but whatever else happened at the encounter between the saint and the druids, it was not the paschal fire which was extinguished. Toleration was accorded thereafter for the teaching of Christianity.

The work of evangelising Ireland was full of peril. St Patrick writes, towards the end of his life: 'Daily I expect either a violent death or to be robbed and reduced to slavery or the occurrence of some such calamity . . . I have cast myself into the hands of Almighty God, for he rules everything; as the Prophet said, "Cast your care on the Lord, and he himself will sustain you" '. His writings, reveal his intense love of humanity second only to his love of God and explain his enormous influence.

Once, for example, the two daughters of King Leoghain, Ethne the Fair and Fedelon the Ruddy, went early to the well to wash. There they found Patrick and his monks, and asked him who they were, and where they came from? Patrick answered, 'It would be better for you to believe in God then to enquire about our race'. The elder girl asked, 'Who is your God and where is he?' Patrick replied: 'Our God is the God of all things, the God of heaven and earth and sea and river. He dwells in heaven and earth and sea and all that are therein. He inspires all things; he quickens all things; he kindles the light of the sun, and the light of the moon. He has a Son, co-eternal with himself, and like him. And the Holy Spirit breathes in them. Father, Son and Holy Spirit are not divided. I desire to unite you to the Son of the heavenly King, for you are daughters of a king of the earth'.

The princesses asked more questions, and were baptised. They asked to see Christ face to face. But Patrick answered, 'You cannot see Christ unless you first taste death, and unless you receive Christ's Body and Blood'. They replied, 'Give us the sacrifice, that we may be able to see the Spouse'. When they had received the sacrifice, they died.

Patrick must have been an old man when he carried out his forty days' fast upon Croagh Patrick. He went to the summit of Mount Aigli and remained there for forty days and forty nights. 'The birds were a trouble to him, and he could not see the face of the heavens, the earth or the sea on account of them; for God told all the saints of Erin, past, present and future, to come to the mountain summit—that mountain which overlooks all others, and is higher than all the mountains of the West—to bless the tribes of Erin, so that Patrick might see the fruit of his labours, for all the choir of the saints of Erin came to visit him there, who was the father of them all.'

The end came when St Patrick was over ninety. He had wished to die in Armagh, when in 444 the cathedral church had been founded, but it is most probable that he died in the year 461 in Saul on Strangford Lough, where he had built his first church.

SHORT VERSION (*St Patrick*)
Patrick, the apostle of the Irish, was probably a Scotsman though both England and Wales have also claimed to be his birth-place. When he was sixteen, he was carried off into slavery in Ireland, but six years later he escaped and finally settled in France. At the age of sixty, Patrick, now a bishop began his missionary labours in Ireland. He started in Ulster and despite much opposition from the King and the Druids many turned to Christ. As an old man Patrick carried out a forty days' fast on the summit of Mount Aigli. The story is told by Tirechan that 'the birds were a trouble to him, and he could not see the face of the heavens, the earth or the sea on account of them; for God told all the saints of Erin, past, present and future, to come to the mountain summit—that mountain which overlooks all others, and is higher than all the mountains of the West—to bless the tribes of Erin, so that Patrick might see the fruit of his labours, for all the choir of the saints of Erin came to visit him there, who was the father of them all'. Patrick died, probably in 461, at Saul on Strangford Lough where he had built his first church.

St Joseph of Nazareth 19 MARCH

Husband of the Blessed Virgin Mary

According to the Gospels Joseph was of royal descent, of the line of David and a just man. The Holy Family presumably were not wealthy, since according to Luke they could only offer a pair of doves at Mary's purification in the temple. They finally settled in Nazareth where Jesus when he grew up followed Joseph's trade as a carpenter. It is thought that St Joseph died before our Lord began his ministry, since there is no allusion to him after that. The cult of St Joseph seems to have begun as late as the fourteenth century. St Gertrude, in 1310, saw in a vision that when the name of St Joseph was pronounced: 'all saints bowed their heads with respect, as a sign of honour to that glorious patriarch, and congratulated him and rejoiced in his incomparable dignity'. It was St Teresa of Avila who largely encouraged devotion to the saint in Western Christendom.

St Cuthbert

20 MARCH

Bishop of Lindisfarne, Missionary, 687

Cuthbert was brought up as a shepherd in Northumbria, and one night when he was about fifteen he saw a vision; a path of light appeared in the dark sky, and a company of angels passed upwards upon it, carrying a soul to heaven. He heard afterwards that on that same night St Aidan had died at Bamburgh. This may have decided the future course of the boy's life, though it must have been some time later that he appeared at the gate of the monastery of Melrose, for we are told that he was mounted and armed when he asked for admission. It is possible that he may have been fighting against the Mercians. Eata, the abbot of Melrose, was absent when Cuthbert presented himself, but he was received by the prior Boisil with the words, 'Behold, a servant of the Lord. Behold, an Israelite in whom there is no guile.' The saint's novitiate was marked by his application to study, watchings and prayer, and by his obedience and abstinence. Some years later the Northumbrian King Alcfrith gave land at Ripon to Eata on which to build a monastery. When it was completed a band of monks accompanied Eata to take possession, and Cuthbert was appointed as guest-master.

Eata and Cuthbert stayed only one year at Ripon. King Alcfrith transferred the abbey to St Wilfred, and those monks who clung to the Celtic usage, as opposed to that of Rome, returned to Melrose. At the death of Boisil, Cuthbert was appointed prior: 'and trained many men in the monastic life with masterly authority and by his personal example'.

At that time the country was ravaged by a disease known as the yellow plague. Cuthbert himself did not escape it, but as he lay ill he was told that the monks were praying for his recovery, and exclaiming that the prayers of such men could not go unheard by God, he rose from his bed and straightway resumed his duties, but his health was affected for the rest of of his life. One evil result of the plague was that the country people had reverted (particularly in remote places) to the use of amulets and charms in panic-stricken efforts to avert the disease. To recall them to Christ, Cuthbert travelled the country from

Berwick to the Solway Firth, on foot and occasionally on horseback. He mostly travelled to out of the way places among the mountains, which by their poverty and natural horrors deterred other visitors, and often remained a week, sometimes a month without returning home. Living among them, he taught the country people heavenly things, both by his words and example.

St Cuthbert would sometimes rise in the night and stand in the sea at prayer. There is a legend of two otters which came out of the water to play at his feet and receive his blessing. Another legend tells how Cuthbert and his companions were saved from starvation by a fish-eagle which settled by a river with its catch. St Cuthbert divided the fish into two pieces and returned one portion to the bird. The town of Kirkcudbright takes its name from the church which was built to mark the spot where St Cuthbert found slices of dolphin's flesh when his party were driven ashore in a snowstorm.

After the Council of Whitby St Eata was called to Lindisfarne to replace St Cuthbert who had resigned, finding himself unable to conform to the Roman use in regard to the disputed date of Easter. St Eata and St Cuthbert had agreed to abide by the findings of the Council and it was their task, as Bishop and Prior of Lindisfarne, to reconcile the monks to the innovations. This difficult task was accomplished by his patience and good temper. 'When he was tired by the bitter taunts of his opponents, he would get up and without a sigh of vexation adjourn the chapter, and the next day, as though he had met no opposition, would repeat his arguments until by degrees he had brought them round to his way of thinking.'

After twelve years, in 676, he obtained permission of the abbot to retire in solitude to an islet off Holy Island, probably the one traditionally named St Cuthbert's Isle. Later he moved to a desolate island of the Farne group where, with the help of the brethren, he built a cell and an oratory, surrounded with a wall so high that he could see nothing but the sky. To these was added a guest-house at a later date. Although the island was waterless and uninhabited, St Cuthbert found a spring, and grew enough barley to support himself. Bede relates that he kept the birds from his barley by preaching to them. The wild fowl of the island became known as St Cuthbert's birds; he tamed them and promised that they should never be disturbed. He is often represented in art with a bird, and more seldom with otters at his feet.

In 685 St Cuthbert yielded to the entreaties of King Egfrid and consented to accept a bishopric. He agreed to change diocese with St Eata, Eata becoming Bishop of Hexham, and Cuthbert Bishop of Lindisfarne, with charge of the monastery. He was consecrated in York Minster by St Theodore, Archbishop of Canterbury, on Easter Day, 685. His episcopate of two years was harassed by another outbreak of plague, during which he went fearlessly about his see, ministering to the sick and dying, and performing many miracles of healing.

A few days after Christmas Day, 686, St Cuthbert returned to Farne Island, knowing that the end was at hand. Two months later he was seized with a mortal sickness. For five days before his death stormy weather made it impossible for anyone to approach the island, but the Abbot Herefrid arrived in time to receive his last instructions and his message to the brethren: 'Be of one mind in your councils, live in peace with other servants of God: despise none of the faithful who seek your hospitality: treat them with kindly charity, not esteeming yourselves better than others who have the same faith and often live the same life. But hold no communion with those who err from the unity of the Catholic faith. Study diligently, carefully observe the canons of the fathers, and practise with zeal that monastic rule which God has deigned to give you by my hands. I know that many have despised me, but after my death it will be found that my preaching has not deserved contempt'.

Bede says of St Cuthbert: 'Above all else, he was afire with heavenly love, unassumingly patient, devoted to unceasing prayer, and kindly to all who came to him for comfort. He regarded the labour of helping the weaker brethren with advice as equivalent to prayer, remembering that he who said, "Love the Lord your God", also said, "Love your neighbour". His self-discipline and fasting were exceptional, and through the grace of contrition, he was always intent on the things of heaven'.

As a young man Cuthbert joined the monastery at Melrose eventually becoming Prior and according to Bede, 'trained many men in the monastic life with masterly authority and by his personal example'. When the country people of Northumbria were returning to pagan spells, as a result of yellow plague, Cuthbert, who had himself fallen prey to the disease, toured the area recalling them to Christ. It was after the Council of Whitby that Cuthbert went to Lindisfarne charged with the task of reconciling those who wished to stick to the usage of the Celtic Church with those who desired the reforms of Whitby. In 676 Cuthbert retired to an islet off Holy Island and thence to an island of the Farne group. Nine years later he was consecrated Bishop of Lindisfarne but his episcopate only lasted two years, for he returned to his Farne island after Christmas Day and died there in 687.

Thomas Ken

Bishop of Bath and Wells, 1711

King James II was once unwise enough to have seven bishops imprisoned simply because they refused to read the Declaration of Indulgence whereby certain posts hitherto preserved for members of the established Church of England were made open to anyone. James was a Roman Catholic and he was obviously hoping that by systematically appointing Catholics to various jobs he could slowly reverse what had happened at the Reformation. Seven bishops refused to read the Declaration and so were sent to the Tower. At their subsequent trial in June 1687 they were all found Not Guilty and promptly released. Ironically in 1690 after the revolution of 1688, one of the seven Thomas Ken a man of great holiness who was then Bishop of Bath and Wells was removed from office because along with other bishops and priests he refused to take an oath of allegiance to King William III. It was not that they thought James a better King, but on the grounds that they had already taken an oath of loyalty to King James II and could not do the same to another while James lived. Thus for a few years there were two Anglican jurisdictions in England. Those who could not in conscience take the oath were known as Non-jurors and were often suspected of conspiracy. Having been ejected from their livings they frequently kept themselves by becoming tutors in noble households. Thomas Ken went to live with Lord Weymouth and his family at Longleat, where visits to friends apart, he remained for the last twenty years of his life, and died on 19 March 1711.

Thomas Cranmer
Archbishop of Canterbury, Martyr, 1556

It was Henry VIII's desire to divorce his first wife, Catherine of Aragon, which led to Cranmer being brought to the King's notice. Till then Thomas had lived a quiet life of a scholar at Cambridge, where, despite the regulations, he had married, though his wife died in childbirth two years afterwards. Henry gave him the job of seeing the question of his marriage debated in the university, and doubtless chose him because he hoped for a favourable judgement. In 1529 Cranmer was part of an embassy sent to Rome, and in 1533 was consecrated Archbishop of Canterbury. As Archbishop Thomas began the proceedings which ended in Henry's divorce from Catherine, and while no one would dispute Thomas' good faith, it is difficult to see much good in the Tudor tyrant. Henry had married Catherine after a papal dispensation anyway which in Thomas' eyes the Pope had had no business issuing in the first place. Under Henry and with greater speed under his son Edward VI, Thomas gradually led the Church along the path of the Reformers. In 1549 the first Book of Common Prayer was published providing for all the Church's worship in English. In that Book, Cranmer reveals the great treasure he has given to the English speaking world. No one has been able to translate the old Latin collects so beautifully. They have a timeless quality and are still in use throughout the English speaking world. When Mary, daughter of Catherine of Aragon, ascended the throne, Thomas prepared for the worst. Mary had remained not simply unswerving to the Roman See; she had all the fire of a once persecuted zealot. Thomas was accused of heresy. After a lengthy trial he recanted in sorts, but afterwards he withdrew his recantation saying, 'forasmuch as my hand offended in writing contrary to my heart, therefore my hand shall first be punished. For if I come to the fire it shall be first burned'. He was burned in Oxford 21 March 1556.

Annunciation of our Lord to the Blessed Virgin Mary   25 MARCH

Christians through the ages have delighted in honouring her whom they call 'our Lady'. Mary's response, 'I am the Lord's servant; as you have spoken, so be it', marked the beginning of our Salvation through Jesus Christ. The Gospel accounts make it quite clear that Mary took a long time to understand what was happening but she was there at the foot of the Cross. Tradition has it that her son appeared to her first after the Resurrection, but she was certainly present at Pentecost. Nothing definite is known of her subsequent life. One tradition says that she died at Jerusalem; another that she accompanied St John to Ephesus and was buried there. The Feast of the Assumption, 15 August, is the traditional date of her death, and there is a legend that when the Apostles opened the tomb they found it empty and filled with lilies and roses. The story is of late date, and probably arose to account for the popular belief that her body was taken or assumed into heaven. Other feasts kept in her honour occur on 2 February, 31 May and 8 September.

John Keble

Priest, Pastor, Poet, 1866

On 22 July 1833 John Keble published under the title *National Apostasy* the text of the Assize Sermon he had preached at Oxford the previous week. Keble had been infuriated by the cavalier approach of the government towards the bishoprics of the Anglican Church in Ireland. While we might have more sympathy with the government of the day, yet we can agree with John Henry Newman who wrote, 'I have ever considered and kept this day as the start of the religious movement of 1833'. Keble's sermon proved to be the beginning of what is usually called the Oxford Movement, when the Church of England began to rediscover her Catholic heritage. Soon afterwards, Keble, along with Pusey and Newman and others, started a series of *Tracts for the Times* in which they endeavoured to show how the Anglican Church by its Prayer Book and practice had never ceased to hold Catholic truth. Naturally in Victorian, and in parts of very Protestant, England, they provoked much abuse, being accused of Popery. Some of them, including Cardinal Newman, did submit to the Roman See but Keble spent his life serving his Lord within the Church of England. He died on 29 March 1866. He has left behind a book of poems, *The Christian Year*, which when it was published in 1827 helped to gain him the post of Professor of Poetry at Oxford. There are not many great poems among them, but a few have found permanent places in our hymn books including that well loved, 'Blest are the pure in heart'.

Saints and Martyrs of the Americas

This commemoration might include:

Martyrs of North America, *1642–1649*

Early missionary work in Canada among the native Indian tribes was begun by the French. Among them were eight priests who were put to death by the Iroquois over a period of seven years. The horrible sufferings of two of them in particular, St John de Brébeuf and St Gabriel Lalemant, and their courage in the face of it are a source of much inspiration. All of the men were Jesuits. Their feast day is 26 September.

St Rose of Lima, *Virgin, 1617*

Rose was the daughter of Spanish colonists in Peru. She was a very pretty child but she hated being told so, for she feared the sin of vanity. As a young woman and for ten years despite the wishes of her parents, now fallen on hard times, she avoided marriage and eventually became a Sister of the Third Order of the Dominicans. She died after a long illness in 1617 and is the first Catholic canonisation of the New World. Her feast is 30 August.

St Elizabeth Seton, *Founder of a Community, 1821*

First native born US citizen to be canonised by the Roman Catholic Church, Elizabeth was widowed after only nine years of a happy marriage, in 1803. She had been brought up as an Episcopalian, but in 1805 she became a Roman Catholic and in that Church she founded many parochial day schools. She and her sisters of the religious community she founded were also responsible for teacher training, parochial visiting, and caring for orphans. She died when she was forty-seven years old.

Other Saints and Martyrs from the Americas include, in this century: William Porcher DuBose, St Frances Xavier Cabrini, Jim Elliott and Companion Martyrs, Martin Luther King.

William Law

Mystic and Non-juror, 1761

He was one of those clergymen of the Church of England who found themselves unable to take the oath of allegiance to the Hanoverian dynasty of England. Very little is known of his life but his book *A Serious Call to a Devout and Holy Life* is a classic on the spiritual Life and still read today. It was first published in 1728 and among others it brought him the friendship of John and Charles Wesley. A year before his book came out, William had become tutor to Edward Gibbon at Putney. In 1740 he retired to his birth place, Kings Cliffe, near Stamford. In his last years he seems to have led a life that was very similar to that of a monastery. He was a stout defender of the poor and shared his food with them every day, so much so that the local vicar once preached a sermon denouncing such indiscriminate charity. Law died on 9 April 1761.

St Anselm

*Archbishop of Canterbury, Teacher of the Faith,
1109*

Anselm was born at Aosta, in Piedmont, in 1033. His early
attempt to enter a monastery was unavailing, as the abbot
feared his father's displeasure. Disappointed of his vocation, he
turned for consolation to the pleasures of the world, but he was
a natural scholar and when, at the death of his mother, his
father's harshness drove him from home, he went to study in
Burgundy. Three years later he was at Bec in Normandy,
where the abbey, under its prior Lanfranc, was a famous seat of
learning. Anselm became a monk, and stayed at Bec for thirty
years, as prior, and later as abbot, in succession to Lanfranc his
master, who became his lifelong friend.

During his years at Bec, Anselm came to be acknowledged as
the foremost theologian of his day, and the greatest
metaphysician since Augustine. He was an inspired teacher,
and, to quote Baring-Gould: 'His love and interest were for the
younger men, for minds not yet dulled to the wonder and great
ends of living.' To them he showed a forbearance and
understanding far in advance of his period. His biographer
Eadmer gives an account of a discussion between Anselm and
an abbot who complained that his pupils, perverse and
incorrigible to start with, instead of profiting from beatings
conscientiously administered by day and by night, merely
became dull and brutal. Anselm replied: 'If you planted a young
tree in your garden and then confined it on every side so that its
branches could not spread, would it not turn out a strange,
misshapen thing when at last you set it free; and through your
own fault? These children have been planted in the garden of
the Church to grow and bear fruit for God, but you cramp
them so with threats and punishments that their tempers are
spoilt and they become sullen and resist all correction.'

At Bec, an unruly monk called Osbern, who resented
Anselm's promotion, was led to submission by gentle methods,
and then subjected to sterner discipline until he returned to
strictness of life. Anselm nursed him in his last illness, and after
his death wrote at the conclusion of a letter to his friend

Gundulf: 'Remember me, and forget not the soul of Osbern, my beloved. If I seem to burden you too much, then forget me, and remember him.'

Anselm wrote two treatises which place him among the great and original thinkers of Christendom; the *Monologium*, an exposition of the nature of God, revealed by unassisted reason, and the *Proslogium*, which followed it, with the argument that the existence of the idea of God in the human mind itself proves the reality of the idea, thus answering the question raised by the earlier treatise.

Sometimes Anselm had to visit England, where his abbey held property. Through his friendship with Lanfranc, then Archbishop of Canterbury, he became known to all the principal men in the kingdom. He was sympathetic to the English, and at the same time held the respect of the occupying Normans. Of his relations with that difficult man, William the Conqueror, it was said: 'To all others so harsh and terrible, in Anselm's presence he seemed, to the bystanders, another man, so gracious and easy of speech.' When William was dying at Rouen he sent for Anselm to confess him.

For three years after Lanfranc's death, the see of Canterbury was kept vacant. William Rufus refused to appoint a successor and possessed himself of the revenues. But in 1092 he was seized with an illness, during one of Anselm's visits to England, and in terror of death promised to reform and to appoint an archbishop. He nominated St Anselm who was at his bedside, and so reluctant was Anselm to accept the office that the pastoral staff had to be forced into his hand and he was carried to the cathedral.

The king recovered, and immediately tried to extort from Anselm 1000 marks in payment for his nomination. Not only was the demand refused, but the new archbishop pressed Rufus to fill the many vacant abbeys and permit the convening of synods to legislate against abuses. The king angrily refused both requests.

Another difficulty arose; it was necessary for a new archbishop to receive the pallium from the reigning Pope. But at that time both Urban II and Clement claimed the chair of St Peter, and while France and Normandy acknowledged Urban, England, at the direction of Rufus, acknowledged neither.

Anselm insisted that the Great Council should be called to settle the matter, but the bishops refused to commit themselves, beyond advising Anselm to waive his right of acknowledging Urban, and to submit himself to the king's will in the matter. Anselm replied: 'In the things that are God's, I will render obedience to the Vicar of St Peter; and in those which belong of right to my lord the king I will render him both faithful council and service.' But although the bishops had deserted Anselm, the barons were not prepared to countenance a precedent so dangerous to their privileges. In the end they carried the day, and Rufus, who could not afford to alienate them, was obliged to restore Anselm to favour.

After a dispute with the king over feudal service, Anselm travelled to Rome to seek advice from Urban II. As a result, William was threatened with excommunication, but Anselm remained in exile until the king's death made it possible for him to return to his see. During a peaceful period in a monastery in Campania, he finished his famous book, *Cur Deus Homo*, a treatise on the Incarnation.

Anselm returned to England to be welcomed joyfully by king and people. But Henry I insisted on the right of investiture, and Anselm resisted his claim. Again the saint journeyed to Rome, where Henry sent a deputy to present his case. Pope Paschal II confirmed the decision of Urban, at which Henry forbade the archbishop to return, and confiscated his revenue. Threatened with excommunication Henry agreed to meet Anselm in Normandy, and at their meeting they were reconciled.

The king agreed to renounce the right of investiture to bishoprics or abbeys, and Anselm, with papal consent, agreed that English bishops should be free to do homage for their temporal possessions. Henry not only kept his word in the matter of investiture, but during an absence in Normandy appointed Anselm to act as his regent.

St Anselm died on 21 April 1109, in his seventy-sixth year. He was buried in Canterbury cathedral, next to Lanfranc, but his body was afterwards removed to the chapel which now bears his name.

Before he became Archbishop of Canterbury in 1092, Anselm had for thirty years been a monk, prior and later Abbot of the Benedictine Abbey at Bec. He was acknowledged as the foremost theologian of his day, but was also a gentle and inspiring teacher, showing a forebearance and understanding far ahead of the times. His duties as abbot brought him to England and explains how William Rufus nominated him as archbishop in succession to Anselm's great friend Lanfranc. Throughout the reign of both Rufus and his successor, Anselm was constantly having to protect the Church from civil authority and it was during one of his several exiles that he wrote his most famous book on the Incarnation. He died at Canterbury and was buried in the cathedral in 1109.

St George

Patron Saint of England, Martyr, 4th Century

The legends which surround St George tend to obscure the few historical facts, which establish beyond doubt that he was a martyr who met his end at Dispolis (Lydda) in Palestine, at the time of the persecutions of the Emperors Diocletian and Maximian. He has been confused with the Arian bishop, George of Cappadocia, who in 362 was torn to pieces by his flock, after an infamous career of oppression, extortion and various malpractices. But he is included in a list of saints published in 495 by Pope Gelasius, 'whose names are justly reverenced among men, and whose acts are known only to God'. A ruined church in Syria has an inscription to St George, it alludes to him as a holy martyr and is dated 346, fifteen years before the death of the Arian George. A sixteenth century author mentions that Constantine the Great dedicated a church to St George the Martyr in 330. Persia has the remains of many churches dedicated to him, and one in Urmia has a clump of rose bushes fifty yards square, sacred to the saint, which may account for his association with the rose. It is not clear how St George came to be adopted as the patron saint of England, but we probably owe him to the Crusades.

St Mark the Evangelist   25 APRIL

St Mark the Evangelist is generally believed to be the John Mark, cousin of Barnabas, son of the Mary, whose house was one of the meeting places of the brethren at Jerusalem. As he was related to Barnabas, a Levite and a Cypriot, he was probably of Levitical origin.

He accompanied Paul and Barnabas on their first missionary journey, but left them at Perga, and returned to Jerusalem. Some scholars think that he may have disapproved of St Paul's preaching to the Gentiles, others that he feared the dangers of the way. St Paul evidently considered him unreliable and refused to take him on the mission to Cilicia and Asia Minor. Barnabas wanted to include Mark, and his difference of opinion with Paul was so serious that they parted company. Mark sailed with Barnabas to Cyprus, while Paul with Silas visited Syria and Cilicia.

St Paul writes of him ten or twelve years later as a fellow-labourer at Rome, and in his letter to Philemon bids the Colossians receive him if he should visit them, as he evidently intended to do.

It is tradition that Mark acted as an interpreter for Peter at Rome. It was at Rome that Mark wrote the second Gospel, probably between the years 65 and 70, and is said to have been helped to compile it by Peter. Some scholars doubt that Mark was ever one of our Lord's disciples, but others are inclined to identify him with the young man who followed our Lord after his arrest, and who fled naked when the young men laid hold on him, leaving his linen garment in their grasp. Certainly St Peter in his First Epistle includes 'Mark, my son' in his salutation.

It is a tradition, probably true, recorded by Eusebius and also in the Latin preface in the Vulgate to St Mark's Gospel that Mark became the Bishop of Alexandria. The Roman Martyrology says of him that he 'was the disciple and interpreter of Peter the Apostle. He was sent for to Rome by the brethren and there wrote a gospel, and having finished it, went into Egypt. He was the first to preach Christ at Alexandria and formed a church there. Later he was arrested for his faith in Christ, bound with cords and grievously tortured by being dragged over stones. Then, while shut up in prison, he was comforted by the visit of an angel, and finally, after our Lord himself had appeared to him, he was called to the heavenly kingdom in the eighth year of Nero'.

SHORT VERSION (*St Mark*)

St Mark the Evangelist is generally believed to be the John Mark, cousin of Barnabas, and son of Mary whose house was one of the meeting places of the brethren at Jerusalem. He accompanied Paul and Barnabas on their first missionary journey, but left them at Perga, and returned to Jerusalem. Some scholars think that he may have disapproved of St Paul's preaching to the Gentiles, others that he feared the dangers of the way. St Paul evidently considered him unreliable and refused to take him on the mission to Cilicia and Asia Minor. Barnabas wanted to include Mark, and his difference of opinion with Paul was so serious that they parted company. Mark sailed with Barnabas to Cyprus, while Paul with Silas visited Syria and Cilicia. However St Paul is writing about him favourably ten or twelve years later. Tradition has it that Mark was with Peter in Rome and that his Gospel is in part Peter's. Mark is said to have become Bishop of Alexandria where he was martyred during Nero's persecution.

St Catherine of Siena

Mystic, 1380

St Catherine was born in Siena on the feast of the Annunciation, 1347, the youngest of a family of twenty-five children born to a prosperous dyer, Giacomo Benincasa and his wife Lapa. Their house, in the street del'Oca, is preserved to this day.

Catherine is said to have been a merry little girl, with a great devotion to our Lady. As a child of six she would sometimes kneel on every step of the staircase and repeat a Hail Mary on her way up or down stairs. At the same age she had a mystical experience; she was returning to her home with her brother Stephen after a visit to a married sister. The boy, who was walking ahead, turned round to see the small Catherine far behind, gazing into the sky, so absorbed by what she saw there that his calls were unheard. When he came back for her and pulled her by the hand, she started, and exclaimed, 'If you could have seen the beautiful thing which I saw, you would not have done that.'

From that day Catherine's vocation was sealed. She put away her childish things and turned to the world of prayer and solitude; a world in which she was so much at home that she could say later that God had taught her to build a refuge in her own soul in which she could dwell at peace, where no storm could disturb her. She came to have need of such a refuge, for when she approached marriageable age her parents deprived her of all privacy and peace, and filled her life with minor persecutions in their efforts to turn her from the religious life. She announced that she would never marry, and with her own hand cut off her golden-brown hair. At last her parents realised that opposition was useless, and she was allowed the use of a small room in which she prayed, fasted and slept upon boards. She joined the Third Order of St Dominic, assumed the habit, and increased the severity of her mortifications. For three years she lived as a recluse in one room, sometimes consoled by visions, at other times tormented by carnal images and temptations, feeling herself abandoned by God. After one such experience of desolation she asked, 'Where were you, Lord,

53

when my heart was filled with impurity?' and the answer came, 'I was in your heart, strengthening you by my grace.'

On Shrove Tuesday, 1366, a time of festival, when Catherine was at prayer, our Lord appeared to her with his mother. Our Lady took Catherine's hand and held it out to her Son, who placed a ring upon it to mark her union with him. Soon afterwards Catherine knew herself called to leave her recluse life and devote herself to the welfare of others. She began to nurse in the hospitals, as the other Tertiaries of her order were expected to do, but she chose to minister to the most repulsive and unrewarding cases, undeterred by ingratitude, abuse and slander.

Although Catherine was acclaimed as a saint by many, she was sharply criticised by others, and once she was summoned to appear before the Chapter General of the Dominicans, but the charges against her must have been dismissed. Her activities were not confined to nursing. She regularly visited the condemned and was so successful in converting those who sought her council that three Dominicans were detailed to hear the confessions of penitents whose consciences she had aroused. She was often resorted to as a peacemaker.

A band of disciples from all walks of life gathered about St Catherine, among them her own confessors, and the painter Andreo Vanni, to whom we owe her portrait. Her director, the blessed Raymond of Capua, became her biographer. In a severe outbreak of plague, she nursed the victims with unremitting devotion, and prepared for death those who were doomed. When Pope Gregory XI called for another crusade against the Turks, Catherine gave him her energetic support and entered into correspondence with him. Her influence thereafter was not to be confined to spiritual affairs; in 1375 Florence and Perugia, together with other cities, entered into an alliance against the Holy See. Florence was laid under an interdict and Catherine offered to mediate with the pontiff. Her offer was accepted and she travelled to Avignon to intercede with Gregory in person. She had already written him some rather severe letters on the subject, and her mission was unsuccessful, but her journey was not wasted. For seventy-five years the popes had been absent from Rome. After such a period of time at Avignon the papal entourage had become almost entirely French, and many evils, affecting all Europe, had arisen from the division of loyalties. Received in audience by Gregory, Catherine raised the question of the return of the papal court to the Holy City. At a much earlier time Gregory had made a vow to return to Rome, but all his efforts to do so had been defeated by the French cardinals. The vow had been a private undertaking between Gregory and his Maker, never revealed to a living soul; he was therefore both startled and conscience-stricken when Catherine bade him fulfil what he had promised. Impressed by her mystic faculty for penetrating the innermost thoughts of others, he lost no time in redeeming his vow, and the papal court returned to Rome. Catherine went back to Florence, which she found still in the same state of unrest and rebellion. She remained there in considerable personal danger; brisk, cheerful and unperturbed. Ultimately Florence was reconciled to the Holy See by her efforts, but after the death of Gregory.

In spite of her preoccupation with political affairs, and her vast, world-wide correspondence (four hundred of her letters are still extant), her spiritual life preserved its fervent, even tenor, illuminated occasionally by visions. At Siena she wrote a mystical work in four treatises, the *Dialogue of St Catherine*. Her director claimed that she dictated the book under the inspiration of the Holy Spirit. Theologians who had questioned her closely early in her career had been obliged to attribute her knowledge to inspiration from a divine source. It has been said of her that in all her works she was actuated solely by her devotion to Christ's Church, and in that lay her nobility. Two years after the return of Gregory to Rome, the great schism occurred with the election of Urban VI at Rome, and an anti-pope at Avignon, where some French cardinals claimed Urban's election illegal. The Christian world was split into two factions, and Catherine flung herself into the struggle to obtain recognition for Urban. She called upon rulers all over Europe to support him, advising Urban himself in the conduct of his campaign, and rebuking him for his harshness which alienated his supporters. Urban kissed the rod and summoned Catherine to Rome to give him further counsel. She obeyed, but her health had been failing seriously for a long time, and she was in incessant pain, although her cheerful serenity remained unimpaired to the last. On 29 April 1380, St Catherine of Siena died at the age of thirty-three. Her last words were: 'Lord, you call me to you, and I come not in my own merits but only in your mercy, which I ask in virtue of the most precious blood of your dear son. Lord, into your hands I commend my spirit.'

SHORT VERSION (*St Catherine of Siena*)
Catherine was a very forceful young lady. During the thirty-three years of her life she resisted her parent's attempt to get her married; escaped a charge of heresy; told Pope Gregory XI he ought to keep his word and take the papal court back to Rome; kept up a vast correspondence with high and low-born alike, attempted to heal the schism between Pope and anti-pope after the election of Pope Urban VI, and still found time to spend hours in prayer and further hours nursing the sick, or visiting condemned criminals. In this last activity she was so successful that three Dominicans were detailed to hear the confessions of those whose consciences Catherine had aroused. She was born in Siena in 1347 and died in 1380.

St Philip and St James

Apostles

There is little problem over the identity of Philip. According to St John's Gospel, he was the first of the apostles to respond to our Lord's call. He came from Bethsaida and an early tradition has it that it was he who asked Jesus if he might go and bury his father only to be told, 'Let the dead bury their dead'. It was Philip at the feeding of the five thousand who asked Jesus how it was to be done; the Greeks who wanted to see Jesus first approached Philip, and it was he who asked Jesus, 'Show us the Father'. Tradition has it that he preached the gospel in Scythia and Phrygia. Another tradition says that he died by crucifixion. No one knows why he has been linked with St James the Less and there is some confusion over which James anyway. Some say it is James, son of Mary and Cleophas, others James the Lord's brother, who presided at the first Council of Jerusalem, and who tradition says was stoned to death in that city at the instigation of the scribes and Pharisees.

St Athanasius

Bishop of Alexandria, Teacher of the Faith, 373

St Athanasius, Archbishop of Alexandria, described by Cardinal Newman as 'a principal instrument, after the Apostles, by which the sacred truths of Christianity have been conveyed and secured to the world' was born at Alexandria, of Christian parents. At an early age he was familiar with the hermits of the desert, and was a disciple of the greatest of them all, St Antony. In the year 318, Athanasius was made a deacon and appointed secretary to the Bishop of Alexandria, attending him in that capacity at the Council of Nicaea.

The Council had been called by the Emperor Constantine in order that Arius, a priest of Baukalis in Alexandria, might state his case before the assembled bishops of the Catholic Church. He had already been excommunicated by a council of Egyptian bishops, and at the Council of Nicaea the sentence was confirmed, and the confession of faith which came to be known as the Nicene Creed was discussed and established.

At the death of Alexander, Athanasius succeeded him, inheriting from his master a huge diocese torn by dissents, heresy and semi-heresy, in which his efforts towards unity were unable to prevail against the opposition which met him on all sides. One of his first actions was to appoint Frumentius as the first Bishop of Ethiopia, where the Church had found a foothold which proved to be lasting. He also visited the Thebaid. Unmoved by threats, and impervious to persuasion, the young Athanasius (he was under thirty) was obliged to oppose the emperor, who had fallen under Arian influence, and ordered him to re-admit Arius to communion.

Athanasius was accused of bribery, treason, extortion and immorality, tried before the emperor and acquitted. Fresh charges were brought against him by his enemies, including that of having murdered a Melitian bishop. The assembly was packed with his adversaries and he was obliged to vindicate himself personally to the emperor. Shortly afterwards he lost favour with Constantine and was banished to Trier, in Belgian Gaul. His exile lasted for two years, until the death of Constantine in 337.

His return to his see was marked by general rejoicing, but Eusebius, the Arian Bishop of Nicomedia whose influence with Constantine had brewed the former trouble, now extended his influence to Constantius, the second son of Constantine, who ruled Alexandria. A further crop of accusations against Athanasius resulted in his deposition in favour of an Arian, a Cappadocian called Gregory, and Athanasius departed to Rome to await the findings of a synod called by the pope, St Julius. The saint was vindicated by the synod and the verdict was later endorsed by the Council of Sardica.

It was impossible for Athanasius to reclaim his see until the death of Bishop Gregory, and his return was delayed until Constantius recalled him in order to please his orthodox brother. His exile had lasted eight years, but his stay in Alexandria was to be short. After the death of the orthodox Emperor Constans, Constantius turned upon Athanasius again, and once more he was obliged to leave Alexandria, this time in such peril of his life that he took refuge in the desert where for six years he was hidden by the monks.

At the death of Constantius, Julian, the apostate emperor, revoked his predecessor's edicts of banishment, but he could not long tolerate the presence of such a powerful opponent of his paganising policy. Again Athanasius was obliged to take refuge in the Thebaid. When the Emperor Jovian succeeded Julian, Athanasius was recalled, only to be banished shortly afterwards by Jovian's successor, Valens. But in response to an outburst of popular feeling among the Egyptians, the emperor was obliged to restore Athanasius to his see. This time he was to remain at Alexandria until his death, seven years later, on 2 May 373.

SHORT VERSION (*St Athanasius*)

Athanasius was exiled from his Archbishopric of Alexandria four times, and at the root of his troubles was his implacable stand against the Arian heresy which denied the divinity of Christ. Athanasius had been secretary to his predecessor during the Council of Nicaea in 325 when the Confession of Faith known as the Nicene Creed was discussed and established. Cardinal Newman described Athanasius as 'a principal instrument after the Apostles by which the sacred truths of Christianity have been conveyed and secured to the world'.

Julian of Norwich

8 MAY

Mystic, c.1417

It is known that at least four people left money in their wills for the support of an anchoress who lived the solitary life, though cared for by a servant, in a cell adjoining the parish church of St Julian in Cornisford at Norwich, opposite a house of Augustinian Friars. Apart from that almost all of what is known of her comes from a book Julian wrote about various visions, which she calls revelations, and which she received on 8 May 1373. She was in bed, her mother was there and Julian thought she was dying. It was at that point that she experienced her visions, and when she recovered she knew she had to write down her *Revelations of Divine Love*. Perhaps the most famous phrase is that which now hangs as a tapestry in St Paul's Cathedral, London, 'All shall be well, and all shall be well and all manner of things shall be well'. Julian saw a hand holding a walnut and she likens this to God and his world. She draws these conclusions, 'God made it, God loves it, God keeps it'. During her lifetime (she was still alive in 1416) many including Margery Kempe, came to Julian for spiritual advice and since her book has become more widely known thousands have gained much help from her.

St Matthias

Apostle

After the death of Judas, St Peter ordained that it was necessary to elect a twelfth apostle. Two candidates were chosen from among the seventy-two disciples who 'bore us company all the while we had the Lord Jesus with us'. The two candidates were Matthias and Joseph, called Barsabas and Justus. Both were qualified to bear witness to the life of Jesus Christ, his death and resurrection. The decision was made by the drawing of lots, and the lot fell upon Matthias. We are told that the first part of his ministry was spent in Judea, and that he was there tried for being a Christian. When the judge wished to give him time to consider renouncing his faith, he answered, 'God forbid that I should repent of the truth that I have truly found and become an apostate.' After this he was stoned and beheaded at Jerusalem. Another tradition holds that he preached in Cappadocia and along the coast of the Caspian Sea, suffering great hardship and ill-usage, and was finally crucified at Colchis.

St Dunstan

Archbishop of Canterbury, 988

St Dunstan was born in 925, the first year of King Athelstane's reign. His father was a thane, and he was educated at Glastonbury, in the neighbourhood of his birth. From Glastonbury he was sent to the king's court. Studious, and probably rather withdrawn, he seems to have made himself so unpopular that he was expelled on a false charge of practising incantations, and flung into a muddy pond with his hands and feet tied.

Dunstan's uncle, Bishop Alphege of Winchester, urged him to enter the religious life. The young man hesitated for some time, but after recovering from a skin complaint, which he believed to be leprosy, he received the habit and later took holy orders. He then returned to Glastonbury.

At Glastonbury Dunstan built himself a cell near the old church, and devoted himself to study, music, metal-work and painting, showing great talent and practising the arts for the glorification of the Church—a manuscript illuminated by St Dunstan is in the possession of the British Museum. King Athelstane died and was succeeded by his brother Edmund the Magnificent. Edmund recalled Dunstan to court, but again he was the victim of intrigue and obliged to leave. Soon afterwards the king had a miraculous escape from death while hunting on the Mendips; the stag plunged over the gorge with the hounds at his heels, and the king's horse all but followed them. In gratitude to God for his escape Edmund repaired the injustice committed against Dunstan. He recalled him to court and later appointed him Abott of Glastonbury in the year 943.

Dunstan immediately set about the reorganisation of the abbey and the restoration of the buildings. He made it an important seat of learning, and his reign at Glastonbury arrested the decline of monastic institutions and ushered in a new era in the religious life of England.

Less than seven years after his accession, Edmund was murdered, and was buried at Glastonbury. He was succeeded by his brother Edred, his own sons, Edwy and Edgar, being too young to rule. Edred turned to Dunstan for advice, and adopted his revolutionary ideas for the reform of the secular clergy, the control of cathedrals and abbeys by monks, and the conciliation of the Danish settlers. His supporters were to be found chiefly in East Anglia and the north, and he became their acknowledged leader. But he met with bitter opposition among the victims of his reforms, and the West Saxon nobles were his implacable enemies.

Edred was succeeded at his death by his nephew Edwy, a boy of sixteen, already in love with a close kinswoman named Elgiva. She was a beauty, and her relations with Edwy were lasting, but the tie of blood was too close to admit of their marriage within the laws of the Church. When, at his coronation feast, Edwy absented himself to visit her in her mother's apartment, the guests were enraged at this breach of decorum, and St Dunstan and the Bishop of London followed the king and brought him back to the banquet. Edwy never forgave this humiliation, and with the delighted assistance of Dunstan's enemies, later drove the saint into exile and confiscated his property. St Dunstan took refuge in Flanders, at Ghent, where he was able to observe in a Benedictine monastery continental monasticism at its most vigorous.

North of the Thames the kingdom broke out in rebellion against Edwy and chose Edgar as king. Edgar immediately summoned St Dunstan and bestowed upon him the bishoprics of Worcester and London, an uncanonical measure probably justified by the emergency of the time. At Edwy's death, two years later, the kingdom was united under Edgar, and Dunstan was appointed Archbishop of Canterbury. He was also created a legate of the Holy See, and with this further authority he embarked upon a campaign of reform and restoration which was to influence the English Church for many centuries. His reforms were not confined to the ecclesiastical sphere; distinguished laymen were subject to severe discipline, and King Edgar himself suffered a seven-year penance for the crime of dishonouring a nun.

After the death of Edgar, Dunstan continued to control the state during the short reign of Edward the Martyr, but after the accession of Ethelred Dunstan retired to Canterbury and took no further part in politics. His greatest interest and pleasure lay in the cathedral school. Centuries afterwards its scholars would invoke 'sweet St Dunstan' to mitigate punishment. On the feast of Ascension in the year 988 St Dunstan celebrated mass and announced his impending death to the congregation. After dining in the refectory he went to the cathedral to choose his burial place, and two days later, on 19 May he died.

SHORT VERSION (*St Dunstan*)

In 943 Dunstan was appointed Abbot of Glastonbury by King Edmund. He was no stranger for he had been educated there as a boy and had also begun his monastic life in the Abbey. Dunstan reorganised the Abbey, restored many of its buildings and made it an important seat of learning. On the accession of King Edred, Dunstan became an important adviser at court but was later driven into exile in Flanders. He was recalled by King Edgar who made him Archbishop of Canterbury, and once again the Church and State felt his reforming zeal. When Ethelred became King, Dunstan took no further part in politics and died on 19 May 988.

John and Charles Wesley   24 MAY
Priests, Poets, Teachers of the Faith, 1791, 1788

Of the two brothers born at Epworth Rectory to Samuel and Susanna Wesley, John is the more famous for his lengthy preaching tour, but Charles' words are more frequently on the lips of present day Christians, for he wrote most of their hymns. When John was only six, he was barely rescued from the fire that burnt down the Rectory, and afterwards described himself as a brand snatched from the burning. At University both of them were founder members of a group nicknamed the Holy Club who regulated their lives in accordance with the precepts of William Law. Among other things, they went to Holy Communion once a week, a practice almost unheard of in the Church of England, and undertook various works of mercy. They were subjected to much mockery and called Oxford Methodists, which name has now become the honoured title of a branch of Christendom. In 1735 they went out to the Colony of Georgia under the auspices of the SPG, hoping for an opportunity to work and preach among the Indians. They returned, disillusioned after two years. In their journeys they had met some Moravian Christians and this had left both of them feeling despondent with their spiritual state. Charles was sick and in bed. It was there on Whit Sunday that Charles experienced his acceptance by God in a totally new way. Three days afterwards, on 24 May, his brother John's heart, as he later put it, 'was strangely warmed' while he listened to a sermon. From then onwards John began a constant ministry of preaching, especially to the poor, which made him claim that the world was his parish. He was not welcomed by the established Church, and so gradually preaching houses were built around the country. John Wesley insisted that he had never left the Church of England to found a new Church, but that is in fact what happened. Charles supported his mission and also wrote hundreds of glorious hymns, which became an essential adjunct to their work, but he finally broke with John's teaching when his brother, although not a bishop, began to ordain men himself for their congregations in America.

The Venerable Bede

Priest, Monk of Jarrow, 735

St Bede, 'father of English history', wrote of his early life: 'At the age of seven I was, by the care of my relations, given to the most reverend Abbot Benedict (St Benedict Biscop) and afterwards to Ceolfrid to be educated. From that time I have spent my whole life in the monastery of St Peter and St Paul at Wearmouth and Jarrow devoting all my efforts to the study of the Scriptures, and amid the observance of monastic discipline and the daily charge of singing in the Church it has ever been my delight to learn or teach or write. In my nineteenth year I was admitted to the diaconate and in my thirtieth to the priesthood—both by the hands of the most reverend Bishop John (St John of Beverley) and at the bidding of Abbot Ceolfrid. From the time of my ordination up till my present fifty-ninth year I have endeavoured, for my own use and that of the brethren, to make brief notes upon the Holy Scriptures either out of the works of the venerable fathers or in conformity with their meaning and interpretations.'

Except for brief visits to other monasteries, Bede's life appears to have been spent entirely at Wearmouth and Jarrow, his time divided between study and the instruction of the 600 monks. An account of his last days has come down to us from his disciple, the monk Cuthbert. He was taken ill a fortnight before Easter, 735. Between Easter and Ascension he was engaged in translating St John's Gospel into English, as well as a collection of notes from St Isidore, saying, 'I will not have my pupils read what is false, or unprofitably labour on this after my death.'

On Rogation Tuesday he was worse, and urged his secretary, 'Go on quickly: I do not know how long I shall hold out and whether my Maker will soon remove me.' He spent the night awake, in thanksgiving, and began to dictate the last chapter of St John. At the ninth hour he said to his scribe, 'There are some articles of value in my chest, such as peppercorns, napkins and incense; run quickly and bring the priests of the monastery to me that I may distribute among them the gifts which God has bestowed on me.' When this was done he entreated their prayers and said, 'You shall see my face no more in this life. It is time for me to return to him who formed me out of nothing. The time of my dissolution is at hand; I desire to be dissolved, and to be with Christ.' In the early evening his scribe 'said, "Dear master, there is yet one sentence not written." Bede answered, "Then write it quickly now." Soon after the boy said, "It is finished. The sentence is now written." He replied, "It was well said, it is finished. Raise my old head in your arms, that I may look once more at the happy, holy place, where I used to pray, that sitting up in my bed, I may call on my Father." And thus on the pavement of his little cell, singing, "Glory be to the Father, and to the Son, and to the Holy Spirit", he breathed his last.'

The title Venerable is a term of respect formerly bestowed upon distinguished members of religious orders, but there are two legends to account for its bestowal upon St Bede. According to one, a mischievous boy led the saint, in the blindness of old age, to preach to a congregation composed of large stones. When Bede had finished his sermon the stones cried, 'Amen, Venerable Bede'.

The other tells how a disciple fell asleep as he searched his mind for an adjective which would aptly describe Bede in an epitaph. When he awoke, an angel had completed it with the title Venerable.

SHORT VERSION (*The Venerable Bede*)

The Venerable Bede lived his entire life, apart from brief visits to other monasteries in the Benedictine abbey of Wearmouth and Jarrow. His book *Ecclesiastical History of the English People* makes him the father of English history. In the last months of his life, he died in 735, he was engaged in translating St John's Gospel into English. Just before Ascension he knew he was dying. The young monk who was his secretary urged him to complete it. 'Dear master there is yet one sentence not written.' Bede answered, 'Then write quickly now.' Soon after the monk said, 'It is finished. The sentence is now written.' He replied, 'It is well said, it is finished. Raise my old head in your arms, that I may look once more at the happy, holy place, where I used to pray, that sitting up in my bed, I may call on my Father.' And thus on the pavement of his little cell, singing, 'Glory to the Father, and to the Son, and to the Holy Spirit,' he breathed his last.

St Augustine

26 MAY

First Archbishop of Canterbury, 605

St Augustine, prior of the monastery of St Andrew, in Rome, was chosen by Pope Gregory the Great to lead thirty monks on a mission to evangelise Anglo-Saxon England.

They set out in the year 596, but were so discouraged by rumours of the savagery of their intended converts that they halted in Provence while Augustine travelled back to Rome to ask St Gregory to recall them. Instead, he rejoined them with St Gregory's instructions to proceed on their mission. The Pope did, however, furnish them with a safe-conduct from the Franks in Gaul, and definite assurances that the English would welcome them. The missionaries landed in Thanet in 597. King Ethelbert, fearing magic, ordered that they should meet him in the open field. They advanced in procession, preceded by the cross, chanting a litany, 'furnished with divine, not magic, virtue'. Ethelbert received them hospitably, giving them permission to preach their gospel and making them free of a dwelling in Canterbury, still known as the Stable Gate.

Once established in Canterbury, the monks were able to use the old church of St Martin, where Ethelbert's Christian queen was accustomed to pray. At Pentecost Ethelbert himself was baptised, and a great number of his subjects followed his example, won by the lives of St Augustine and his monks as much as by their doctrines.

The saint built the monastery of Christchurch on the site of a Roman basilica; this was also to be the site of the present cathedral. He also built the church of St Peter and St Paul, the burial place of the early archbishops. He went to Arles to be consecrated Bishop of the English by St Virgilius.

In 601 Augustine sent two of his monks to Rome to report and to request helpers and guidance on many points. They returned with the pallium for their bishop and a plan for the organization of the English Church. There were to be two archbishops, one at London and one at York. Each was to have twelve suffragans, and Augustine was to be Bishop of London. St Gregory also sent helpers, among whom were St Mellitus, St Justus and St Paulinus. He sent excellent advice on moderation:

'He who would climb to a lofty height must go by steps, not leaps.' He advised respect for local customs, and the grafting of the new Christian observances on to the ancient stock of heathen festivals. The ancient British Church had been driven into Wales and Cornwall, and through lack of communication with the continent still clung to usages which had been abandoned by Rome. In an attempt to secure their co-operation Augustine called a conference with the bishops of the old British Church at St Augustine's Oak, believed to have been at Aust, on the Severn. The bishops were reluctant to depart from their own tradition, and although they were impressed by Augustine's success in the ordeal by miracle (he healed a blind man, where they had failed) they asked for a second conference.

The second conference was equally unsuccessful. The bishops had been advised, in consultation with a hermit, to be guided by Augustine's behaviour. If he rose to greet them they were to hear him submissively, but if he failed in this politeness they might despise him. Unfortunately Augustine did fail, he received them seated. He tried to bargain, offering them liberty to retain all their customs in return for keeping Easter at the same time as the rest of Western Christendom and baptising in the Roman manner. Worse still, he threatened them with divine judgement. The bishops refused to entertain his proposals and declined to acknowledge his authority as their metropolitan. St Augustine died on 26 May 604, seven years after his first landing in England. He was buried in the unfinished monastery church which was to be dedicated to him.

SHORT VERSION (*St Augustine of Canterbury*)

Augustine and his companions, sent from Rome by Gregory the Great, landed at Thanet in Kent in 597. King Ethelbert's Queen was already a Christian, and the missionaries were able to use St Martin's Church where she prayed. By Pentecost the king and a great number of his subjects had been baptised and Augustine was soon to be consecrated Bishop. Later Augustine tried to persuade the bishops of the ancient British Church to co-operate with him but he was rather tactless and they refused. He died seven years after his arrival in England and is buried in Canterbury.

Justin

1 JUNE

Martyr at Rome, c.165

Although Justin was born near Sychem in Samaria his parents were pagans. In his famous *Dialogue with the Jew Tryphon*, Justin records how he tried many philosophies in his search for peace of mind. He became a Stoic, then a follower of Pythagoras, then of Plato. Finally he met an old man who told him, 'To cross the limits of reason, divine help is necessary; this help God has procured for us through the prophets, Christ and the Apostles. Pray, if you wish the gates of light to be opened to you.' Justin took the advice and was given faith. He wrote this dialogue around 135, after he had met Tryphon at Ephesus, and in it he shows how the Old Testament prefigures Christ. It is particularly interesting to note that later on he was to write 'It is a manifest argument of infedility to inquire, concerning the things of God, "How?" or "After what manner?"' (translation by Jeremy Taylor). Justin afterwards went to Rome where he began teaching students the way of life. He was involved in theological controversy which led to his denunciation and subsequent trial and martyrdom.

St Boniface   5 JUNE
Bishop, Missionary, Martyr, 754

St Boniface was born about the year 680 in the neighbourhood
of Crediton in Devonshire. When he was five, he listened to
some monks who were staying at his father's house. They had
returned from a mission to the heathen on the continent, and
Boniface was so impressed by them that he resolved to become
a monk. Although his father had intended him for a secular
career, he gave way to his son's entreaties and Boniface entered
the monastery school near Exeter. At fourteen he passed on to
the abbey of Nursling, in the diocese of Winchester, and
eventually became director of its school. He compiled the first
Latin grammar published in England, and his lectures were
copied out and circulated.

Boniface was ordained at the age of thirty, and although a
career of great promise opened before him in his own country
he knew that his true vocation had been revealed to him as a
child. Paganism reigned throughout northern and central
Europe, and St Willibrord struggled against great odds to
spread the Gospel in Friesland. Boniface obtained a reluctant
permission from his abbot and set out for Germany. He landed
at Duurstede with two companions, but after a few months
they returned to England. The heathen King Radbod was in
conflict with Charles Martel of Gaul, and a persecution of
Christians had broken out. Boniface was welcomed back to
Nursling, and at the death of the abbot the brethren wished to
elect him, but he was not to be turned from his purpose.
Realising that he must have direct authority from the Pope for
his missionary activity, Boniface secured a general commission
to preach the Gospel to the heathen. He crossed the Alps and
journeyed through Bavaria into Hesse.

The death of Radbod made it possible for St Boniface to join
St Willibrord in Friesland, the scene of his earlier attempt. St
Willibrord wished to be able to look on Boniface as his
successor, but the Englishman declined, regarding his
commission as a general one. He returned to Hesse, where his
work was so successful that Gregory consecrated him a
regionary bishop with general jurisdiction over Germany. He

71

also obtained from the Pope a letter to Charles Martel who, as Mayor of the Palace, wielded far more power in Gaul than the king, and was to be the founder of the Carolingian dynasty.

In Hesse he had felled the tree of Geismar, an oak of immense age and girth, sacred to Thor, the god of thunder. Boniface himself made the first strokes of the axe, watched by the devotees of the cult, whom he had summoned to witness the desecration of their sanctuary. After a few blows the great tree trembled and crashed, splitting into four parts. Thor's faithful, who had hoped to the last that St Boniface and his clergy would be struck by lightning, were obliged to admit that their gods were unable to protect their own property. The work of conversion in Hesse proceeded so well that Boniface went on to Thuringia. There he established a monastery, but he found himself short of teachers, and the English monasteries sent him great numbers of monks and nuns to further his work of evangelisation.

Under the last Merovingian kings Christianity in France had become more nominal than actual. Charles Martel had done little to further reform, but at his death his son Carloman was persuaded by St Boniface to call a synod to deal with abuses in his part of his father's territories, which were divided between the two brothers. The next year his brother Pepin called a synod for Gaul, and later a general council of the two provinces was called. The Bishop of Mainz was deposed for killing the murderer of his father, and in 746 Boniface was called on by the Frankish nobles to occupy the vacant see. Pope Zacharias created him primate of Germany and apostolic legate for Germany and Gaul. When Carloman retired into a monastery, Pepin united France under his rule, and he continued to support St Boniface. When he was anointed king at Soissons it was St Boniface who performed the ceremony.

As St Boniface grew old he resigned his see and set out to complete the evangelisation of the Frisians. He consecrated Eoban Bishop of Utrecht, and with Eoban, three priests, three deacons, four monks and forty-one laymen, he sailed down the Rhine and began work among the Frisians who had lapsed since the death of St Willibrord. In the following year they crossed the lake which divides Friesland and penetrated into that part of the country which was still completely unevangelised. Great numbers were converted and Boniface had arranged a confirmation on Whitsun Eve.

On the morning of the appointed day, while the saint was reading in his tent, a hostile crowd descended upon the little encampment. His followers would have defended him, but Boniface refused. 'Let us not return evil for evil; the long-expected day has come, and the time of our departure is at hand. Strengthen yourselves in the Lord, and he will redeem your souls. Fear not those who can destroy the body, but put your trust in God, who will give you an eternal reward, and admit you into his heavenly kingdom.' Their enemies fell upon them, and Boniface was one of the first to perish in the massacre. He is said to have rested his head upon a volume of the Gospels as he awaited the death-blow.

SHORT VERSION (*St Boniface*)
At the age of five, Boniface, born around 680 AD made up his mind to be a monk. His home was in Crediton in North Devon but he entered a monastic school in Exeter. As a young boy he had also decided that he wanted to preach the Gospel in pagan lands and at thirty he set out for Germany. For over thirty years Boniface toiled throughout Germany both breaking new ground and caring as bishop for Christ's flock, particularly for those in the area of the Rhine. As an old man he resigned his see but then set out to evangelise the people of Friesland, where he was martyred on the eve of Pentecost, 754.

St Columba

Abbot of Iona, Missionary, 597

Columba was born in Ulster, probably in Donegal, about the year 521, and was educated at the great monastic schools of Moville and Clonard, with an intervening period of study under a bard in Leinster. He was ordained priest either at Clonard, or later when he was studying at St Mobhi's school at Glasnevin. At the age of twenty-five he returned to Ulster and spent the next fifteen years in preaching and founding monasteries all over Ireland. He was a scholar and delighted in copying manuscripts (he was said to have transcribed three hundred copies of the Gospels) and this brought him into conflict with King Diarmuid. He copied St Jerome's psalter which he had borrowed from his former master, St Finnian. St Finnian claimed the transcript, and the case went before King Diarmuid who decided against St Columba.

Shortly afterwards, while Columba was still angry at the king's decision, Diarmuid's men dragged a fugitive from Columba's protection and slew him, violating the strict laws of sanctuary. It is believed that Columba instigated the war which then broke out between his clan and the followers of King Diarmuid. Three thousand were slain at the ensuing battle of Cuil Dremne and Columba was held to be responsible for their deaths. He was censured, and would have been excommunicated if St Brendan had not intervened. In expiation he accepted exile from his own country, with the purpose of winning for Christ as many souls as had perished in the battle. In the year 563 he embarked, with twelve kinsmen, in a coracle and landed on the island of Iona.

The island, three miles by two, lies on the west coast of Scotland, bleak, flat and featureless, shadowed by the mountains of Mull. The land was given to Columba by the King of Scottish Dalriada, a kinsman of his mother. There he set about building the monastery, and for the first years occupied himself with teaching the Irish-descended Christians of Dalriada. After two years he began his work of conversion among the heathen Picts. He journeyed incessantly into Pictland; he penetrated the castle of the heathen King Brude at

Inverness, and so impressed him that the king held him in great honour for the rest of his days. He also confirmed him in his possession of Iona.

During such time as Columba spent in Iona he occupied himself with prayer, study, transcription and manual labour. He had also to receive a constant stream of visitors of all sorts and conditions. It has been said of him that 'of all qualities, gentleness was precisely the one in which Columba failed the most.' He was as hard on others as on himself, but as he aged those who sought him never failed to find sympathy and help.

St Columba was gifted with second sight and prophesied the fame of the Isle of Iona: 'Unto this place, small and mean though it be, great homage shall yet be paid, not only by the kings and peoples of the Scots, but by the rulers of barbarous and distant nations with their peoples. The saints, also, of other churches shall regard it with no common reverence.'

One day in 597, when the monks came to the church for Matins they found him there. He died before the altar. His attendant Diarmuid raised him, and he made a feeble effort to bless those about him, and so breathed his last.

SHORT VERSION (*St Columba*)
Exiled from his native Ulster, Columba landed on Iona in 563. His troubles at home culminated in a tribal civil war in which three thousand were slain. Columba had been held responsible for the war, and in his exile he vowed to convert as many souls for Christ as had been killed. The remainder of his life was spent in missionary journeys throughout Scotland with occasional periods on Iona which in his day and afterwards was the base for constant missionary endeavour. While on the island, Columba spent his days in prayer, study, copying out the Scriptures and manual labour. He received a constant stream of visitors which is perhaps surprising for he was as hard on others as he was on himself. Gifted with second sight he prophesied the future greatness of Iona and died before the altar of its Abbey in 597 AD.

St Barnabas the Apostle

St Barnabas was a Levite, born in Cyprus. He was originally called Joseph but his name was changed to Barnabas by the disciples, a word meaning 'son of exhortation' or 'consolation' or 'encouragement'. Although he was not one of the twelve, there is authority for supposing him to have been one of the seventy disciples, and he was accepted as an apostle by the early fathers. The first converts at Jerusalem held all property in common, and Barnabas sold land and gave the money to the Apostles.

When St Paul came to Jerusalem after his conversion, the faithful were suspicious of him, and it was Barnabas who took him by the hand and guaranteed his good faith. When it was decided to send someone from the church at Jerusalem to guide the young church at Antioch, Barnabas was chosen. He visited Tarsus to find Paul, and they worked together at Antioch for a year. It was then at Antioch, that the disciples were first called Christians. During a famine in Judea the disciples at Antioch collected relief for their poorer brethren and Barnabas and Paul were chosen to take it to them. After they had carried out their errand they returned to Antioch bringing with them Barnabas's nephew John Mark.

The Antioch Church had many prophets and teachers, and as they worshipped and after prayer and fasting, the two apostles were commissioned by the laying-on of hands, and departed to Seleucia, and from there sailed to Cyprus, taking John Mark with them. After preaching in Salamis in Cyprus, they travelled to Paphos, then to Perga, where John Mark left them to return to Jerusalem and at Antioch in Pisidia they preached to the Jews with little success. At Iconium they were nearly stoned. At Lystra Paul worked a miracle of healing and the people hailed them as pagan gods, Paul as Mercury, and Barnabas as Jupiter, and could barely be restrained from sacrificing to them. But Jews from Antioch and Iconium worked upon the feelings of the mob to such an extent that Paul was stoned, dragged out of the city and left for dead. Next day, however, he went on to Derbe with Barnabas. From Derbe they retraced their steps, confirming and ordaining elders in the new churches, until they reached Antioch in Syria where they had started.

A Council was called at Jerusalem to settle the question of the observance of Jewish rites by Gentile converts. Barnabas and Paul opposed those who wanted all Gentile converts to submit to circumcision, and their view was supported by the Council. The two apostles determined on another missionary expedition to the churches of their foundation, but a difference of opinion caused them to part. Barnabas wished to take John Mark with them, but Paul resented John Mark's desertion in Pamphylia and was determined to leave him behind. After the separation Barnabas is not mentioned again. The fact that Paul sent for John Mark to join him in Rome in the year 60 or 61 suggests that by that time Barnabas had died. There is a tradition that he was stoned to death in Cyprus.

SHORT VERSION (*St Barnabas*)
Barnabas was a very gentle forgiving person. That is how the early Christians gave him his name which means 'son of consolation'. It was Barnabas who introduced the Church in Jerusalem to their one-time persecutor, Saul of Tarsus. It was Barnabas who sought out Paul to be his companion in Antioch. He accompanied Paul on his first missionary journey. Barnabas was prepared to give his nephew, John Mark, who had deserted Paul and Barnabas half-way through their travels, a second chance. It was over John Mark that they parted company and Barnabas with the young man returned to Cyprus, where tradition has it he was stoned to death.

Fathers of the Eastern Church

14 JUNE

St Basil the Great, *Bishop of Caesarea, Teacher of the Faith, 379*

St Basil was born in Caesarea, the capital of Cappadocia. His parents were Christians, the owners of landed property, and his father was a lawyer. Basil was brought up at the country house of his grandmother, St Macrina, and educated at Constantinople and Athens. In Athens two of his fellow-students were Julian, afterwards to become the apostate emperor, and Gregory Nazianzen, son of Gregory, Bishop of Nazianzum. With the latter he was to have a deep and life-long friendship. In 356 he returned to Caesarea as a teacher of rhetoric.

At the age of twenty-nine Basil abandoned his brilliant career and forsook the world which was so full of promise for him. Under the influence of his eldest sister Macrina, and following her example he entered the religious life. She had retired with her widowed mother to a religious community at Annesi, on one of the family estates in Pontus. Her brother travelled through Egypt, Palestine and Syria to visit the great ascetics and solitaries, and finally retired to Pontus to settle in a mountainous retreat separated from Annesi by the river Iris. Basil shared his retreat with some companions, and they established a rule of life which became the pattern for Eastern monastic life. This was the beginning of communal living for monks; hitherto they had lived as solitaries. 'God', Basil said, 'has made us like the members of our body, to need one another's help. For what discipline of humanity, of pity, or of patience, can there be if there is no one for whose benefit these duties are to be exercised? Whose feet will you wash? Whom will you serve? How can you be last of all if you are alone?' His rule, like that of Benedict, who borrowed much from him, united active industry with devotion. One meal only a day was allowed, and that of bread, water and herbs. Sleep was only allowed until midnight, when all rose for prayer. Basil's exclusively monastic life lasted five years.

In 363 Basil was ordained deacon and priest, at Caesarea. But

78

the Archbishop Eusebius was jealous of his influence, differences arose, and Basil retired to Pontus to help in the direction and foundation of new monasteries. But the increasing power of the Arian heresy led him to be recalled to Caesarea, and a reconciliation with Eusebius followed. During a severe famine Basil distributed his entire heritage among the poor. He organised relief on a large scale, and putting on an apron, himself distributed food to the hungry. At the death of Eusebius, Basil was elected to the vacant see.

The reigning emperior, Valens, was an Arian, and at that time was conducting a persecution of orthodox Catholics. His promises and threats availed him nothing in contention with the new Archbishop of Caesarea. Basil refused to compromise with Arians in any way. Valens attempted to banish him, but on three occasions he broke the reed pen as he was signing the edict. After this he abandoned the struggle and left Caesarea in peace.

In spite of his struggle to defend the Church of Caesarea against attacks upon its doctrines and standing, Basil carried out his pastoral duties with furious energy. He preached morning and evening to immense congregations, he supervised his clergy and visited in the most remote and mountainous districts of his diocese. He corrected abuses of all descriptions. He preferred to use gentle methods, but if persuasion could not avail his rebuke could be withering. He forbore to punish where a scolding would serve. No detail escaped his unwearied attention, and his care for the oppressed was unremitting. He founded the Basiliad, a great hospital for the sick poor at the gate of Caesarea, an institution which became celebrated throughout Christendom, and long outlasted its founder.

At the death of St Athanasius, Basil's difficulties increased. He stood alone as the defender of Catholic orthodoxy in its struggle against the increasing forces of Arianism, and his appeals for help were received in Rome with indifference. The victim of jealousy and intrigue, he had been represented as ambitious and self-seeking.

The end of the Arian ascendency in the East was brought about abruptly by the death of Valens, and the accession of his nephew, Gratian, as emperor. But by that time Basil was a dying man, worn out prematurely by chronic ill-health, overwork and disappointment. Many of his letters remain; they are full of sympathy and comfort for the afflictions of other people. Even at the outset of his career, when threatened with the confiscation of his property, banishment and death, he could reply with truth: 'Such threats have no power on one whose sole wealth is a ragged cloak and a few books, to whom the whole earth is a place of pilgrimage, and death a merciful release.' He died at the age of forty-nine, on 1 January 379.

SHORT VERSION (*St Basil*)

St Basil generally is regarded as the founder of monasticism in the Eastern, now Orthodox, half of early Christendom. At twenty-nine, Basil abandoned his wealthy home, gave up his lucrative trading post and with a few companions began to live according to a Rule established by Basil, in a mountainous retreat near Annesi in Pontus. He was ordained in 363 and later became Bishop of his home town of Caesarea. His episcopate was an almost constant battle against the Arian heresy, but he preached morning and evening to immense congregations, he supervised his clergy and visited in the most remote and mountainous districts of his diocese. He corrected abuses of all descriptions. He preferred to use gentle methods, but if persuasion could not avail his rebuke could be withering. He forbore to punish where a scolding would serve. No detail escaped his unwearied attention, and his care for the oppressed was unremitting. He founded the Basiliad, a great hospital for the sick poor at the gate of Caesarea, an institution which became celebrated throughout Christendom, and long outlasted its founder. Basil died at the age of 49 in 379.

This commemoration might also include:

St Gregory of Nazianzum, *Bishop, Teacher of the Faith, c.390*

Gregory became most unwillingly Bishop of Sasima. Among those consecrating him was Basil, his Metropolitan and life-long friend who had appointed him to the job. He did not remain in that insignificant post for long but returned to Nazianzum to act as coadjutor to his father who was bishop there. After his father's death Gregory withdrew to a life of contemplation till the death of Basil. The Arian Heresy then drew him to defend his Orthodox beliefs in Constantinople despite much opposition there.

St Alban

First Martyr of Britain, c.209

The earliest reference to St Alban is by Constantius of Lyons, writing in the fifth century. In his life of St Germanus of Auxerre he states that Germanus, while in Britain, visited the tomb of St Alban, and owed to the intercession of the martyr a smooth passage on his return to Gaul. Alban's story as told by The Venerable Bede runs as follows:

'When the unbelieving Emperors Diocletian and Maximian were issuing savage edicts against all Christians, Alban, as yet a pagan, gave shelter to a Christian priest fleeing from his pursuers. And when he observed this man's unbroken activity of prayer and vigil, he was suddenly touched by the grace of God, and began to follow the priest's example of faith and devotion. Gradually instructed by his teaching of salvation, Alban renounced the darkness of idolatry, and sincerely accepted Christ. But when the priest had lived in his house some days, word came to the ears of the evil ruler that Christ's confessor, whose time of martyrdom had not yet come, lay hidden in Alban's house. Accordingly he gave orders to his soldiers to make a thorough search, and when they arrived at the martyr's house, holy Alban, wearing the priest's long cloak, at once surrendered himself in the place of his guest and teacher, and was led bound before the judge.

'When Alban was brought in, the judge happened to be standing before an altar, offering sacrifice to devils. Seeing Alban, he was furious that he had put himself in such hazard by surrendering himself to the soldiers in place of his guest, and ordered him to be dragged before the idols where he stood. "Since you have chosen to conceal a sacrilegious rebel," he said, "rather than surrender him to my soldiers to pay the well-deserved penalty for his blasphemy against our gods, you shall undergo all the tortures due to him if you dare to abandon the practice of our religion." But Saint Alban, who had freely confessed himself a Christian to the enemies of the faith, was unmoved by these threats, and armed with spiritual strength, openly refused to obey this order' . . . 'Incensed at this reply, the judge ordered God's holy confessor Alban to be flogged by the executioners, hoping to shake the constancy of his heart by torture, since threats had no effect. But, for Christ's sake, he bore the most horrible torments patiently and gladly, and when the judge saw that no torture could break him or make him renounce the worship of Christ, he ordered Alban's immediate decapitation.'

SHORT VERSION (*St Alban*)

The Venerable Bede recounts very fully the death of St Alban, the first martyr for Christ in Britain. In the early years of the fourth century Alban sheltered a Christian priest fleeing from the authorities during one of the several persecutions ordered by successive Roman emperors. Alban watched his guest closely and 'observed this man's unbroken activity of prayer and vigil. He was suddenly touched by the grace of God, and began to follow the priest's example of faith and devotion. Gradually instructed by his teaching of salvation, Alban renounced the darkness of idolatry, and sincerely accepted Christ. But when the priest had lived in his house some days, word came to the ears of the evil ruler that Christ's confessor, whose time of martyrdom had not yet come, lay hidden in Alban's house. Accordingly he gave orders to his soldiers to make a thorough search, and when they arrived at the martyr's house, holy Alban, wearing the priest's long cloak, at once surrendered himself in the place of his guest and teacher, and was led bound before the judge.' Alban was recognised, courageously confessed his faith, and was beheaded near the present site of St Alban's Cathedral.

St John the Baptist 24 JUNE

John the Baptist is the link between the old and the new dispensations. He is both a prophet in Israel, and was popularly regarded as such in his time, and also the forerunner of Messiah. The story of his birth and upbringing are found only in St Luke's Gospel, but all four evangelists report his activities proclaiming the imminence of the Kingdom of God. It is clear that several of our Lord's disciples had first followed John and it would appear that some of them had actually gone to the Jewish communities outside Palestine to preach John's message of repentance and the coming of the Kingdom of God. During his imprisonment by the Tetrarch Herod, John sent a message to Jesus which seems to reveal some doubt in John's mind about our Lord, despite his earlier witness to him at the time of Jesus' baptism by John in the River Jordan. John was eventually beheaded on Herod's orders; but in Christian iconography he and our Lady are frequently depicted in places of honour immediately below Christ.

St Irenaeus 28 JUNE
Bishop of Lyons, Martyr, c.200

As a young man Irenaeus knew Polycarp in his home town of Smyrna but in the year 177 he was in Lyons helping Bishop Pothinus. Thirteen years later he himself became Bishop of Lyons and died in the persecution there of 200. The whole Christian Church owes a great debt to Irenaeus, for it was he who, in the face of Marcion's attempt to alter sacred writings to suit his own theories, first listed many of the books of the New Testament that eventually found a place in the canon of scripture.

St Peter the Apostle 29 JUNE

Throughout the gospel story St Peter, Andrew's brother, stands out as a leading figure, divinely inspired on occasions, at other times liable to act and speak on impulse (a tendency which earned him severe rebukes from his Master), courageous, but not always able to command his courage. Our Lord, who could foresee that Peter would deny him before the servants of the high priest, could still say to him, '. . . you are Peter, and on this rock I will build my Church; and the gates of hell shall not prevail against it.'

After the Ascension he was prominent in the councils of the Apostles, and in building the growing Church in Jerusalem, witnessing before the Sanhedrin, and working miracles. The first miracle of healing recorded in the history of the Christian Church was performed by Peter, the curing of the beggar, lame from birth, who asked alms of Peter and John as they went up to the Temple.

The persecution of the Church at Jerusalem, which followed the martyrdom of Stephen, scattered its members throughout the regions of Judea and Samaria. But Peter and the other Apostles stayed at Jerusalem until the success of Philip's mission to Samaria made it expedient for them to support him there: '. . by praying for those baptised, and laying their hands on them that they might receive the Holy Spirit.'

Peter attended the Council of Jerusalem, called to discuss the reports of Paul and Barnabas, and to decide the conditions under which the Gentiles should be received into the Church. He must have been a powerful influence in the final decision, which was to refrain from forcing Gentiles to observe the law of Moses. At Antioch, he weakened on this point, to the extent of abstaining from eating with Gentiles. For this he was publicly rebuked by Paul.

Early tradition holds that Peter was the first Bishop of Syrian Antioch, occupying the see for two years or more. It is probable that Peter went to Rome during the first imprisonment of Paul, and that he acted as Bishop of the Church at Rome after Paul's release.

A famous legend recounts that Peter, on the eve of martyrdom, allowed his flock to persuade him to escape. At the gate of Rome he met our Lord entering, and said to him, *Domine, quo vadis?*—'Lord, where are you going?' Our Lord replied, 'I am coming to be crucified a second time.' At this, St Peter turned back to meet his death.

By his own desire, St Peter is said to have been crucified head downwards, holding himself unworthy to be crucified in the same manner as our Lord and tradition has it that St Paul was executed on the same day. Peter's body is believed to have been buried in the Vatican, near the Triumphal Way, and to have been removed later to the cemetery on the Appian Way. Pope Cornelius is said to have restored it to the Vatican. Excavations in the present century have established beyond reasonable doubt that the tomb under Peter's basilica is that of the Apostle. It is not possible to be equally certain about the human remains found near the tomb, since it was disturbed by the Saracens in the Middle Ages.

SHORT VERSION (*St Peter*)
St Peter, one of the first disciples is perhaps the most lovable. He was a man of impulse, which gave rise to both his glorious affirmation of faith, 'You are the Christ' at Caesarea Philippi, and to his cowardly denial of his Master outside the high priest's house. It was Peter who first preached the gospel to the Gentiles, yet Peter who backed away from eating with them when there were too many Jews about. Early tradition says he was the first Bishop of Syrian Antioch, and that he later went to Rome, where he was killed. Tradition has it that on the same day as St Paul was beheaded, Peter was crucified and that his own request was that he should be executed upside down, for he thought himself unworthy to suffer in the same manner as his Lord.

St Thomas the Apostle

St Thomas, or Didymus, both names meaning twin, was one of the Twelve, and John's Gospel records four of his sayings, which reveal his character as that of a man who was matter-of-fact and slow to believe, but loving and loyal. When Lazarus lay dead and the other disciples would have dissuaded Jesus from going to Bethany at the risk of his life, but Jesus declared that he would go, St Thomas said, 'Let us also go that we might die with him.' When, in his discourse in the upper chamber, our Lord said, 'Where I am going you know and the way you know', Thomas asked, 'Lord, we know not where you are going so how can we know the way?'

After the Resurrection, when the other disciples said, 'We have seen the Lord,' he replied, 'Unless I see in his hands the print of the nails and thrust my hand into his side, I will not believe.' But when he saw his Lord the next Sunday, he exclaimed, 'My Lord and my God!'

The Apocryphal Acts of Thomas say he went to India and preached. The missionary districts of the Apostles were decided by casting lots. Thomas drew India, and objected, saying, 'I have not strength; I am weak. How can I, a Hebrew, teach the Indians?' In the night the Lord appeared to him, and said, 'Fear not, Thomas; my grace is sufficient for you.' But he still protested, saying, 'Where you want, Lord, but not India.' While he was talking an Indian merchant named Abban appeared. He was in search of a master-carpenter for the service of the Parthian King Gundafor. Our Lord accosted him, and said, 'You are looking for a carpenter. I have a carpenter', and sold Thomas for twenty pieces of silver. Thomas accordingly went to India with Abban.

In India, King Gundafor ordered Thomas to build him a new palace while he was absent on a long journey. When he returned and asked to see the palace, there was nothing to show him. Thomas had given the money for the building to the poor, and had spent his time preaching. He told Gundafor that he should see his palace after his death. The King committed Thomas to prison and ordered him to be flayed alive. At that time, Gundafor's brother died, and saw in Heaven the palace which Thomas had built there for his master. He was permitted to return to the earth to buy it for himself, but Gundafor refused to sell it, and setting Thomas at liberty, was baptised by him, with his brother and many of his people.

When St Francis Xavier began his mission in India, he found a considerable sect of Christians on the Malabar Coast. They called themselves the Christians of St Thomas, and used a Syriac liturgy. They had (and still have) an oral tradition that they were originally converted by the Apostle, who left them to evangelise the Coromandel Coast and was speared to death near Madras.

SHORT VERSION (*St Thomas*)
Thomas the Twin's nickname, 'Doubting Thomas' is a result of the story in John's Gospel which tells how Thomas refused assent to the Resurrection until he had seen the Risen Christ. Tradition has it that he went to India to preach the Gospel and Francis Xavier on his journeys on that sub-continent in the sixteenth century found Christians on the Malabar Coast belonging to a Church that claimed St Thomas as its founder. According to them the Apostle was speared to death near Madras.

Sir Thomas More

Martyr, 1535

Thomas was a lawyer and a very clever one too. He was also a very devout Christian who believed that the unity of the Church, which he found in communion with Rome, was of absolute importance. Henry VIII, recognising Thomas both for his skill as a lawyer and his transparent honesty, made him Lord Chancellor in 1529. However when the King decided to divorce his wife and found that to do so he had first to destroy the authority of the Pope in England, Thomas was unable to agree with him. He resigned his office in 1532 and lived in retirement at his modest home in Chelsea. Up till then, although it was well known that he disapproved of what had been happening, Thomas had not actually said anything in public, nor put anything in writing. In April 1534 he was asked to swear an oath which, amongst other things, accepted the breach with Rome. He refused and so was convicted of treason and beheaded on 6 July 1535.

St Benedict

11 JULY

Abbot of Monte Cassino, c.550

St Benedict was a member of a noble Roman family. With his twin sister Scholastica, he was born in 480 and brought up in the Sabine town of Nursia. At that time the Church was torn by schisms, there was no head of state who was not either heretic, pagan or atheist, and pagan and Arian tribes ravaged the civilised world. The youth of the day imitated the vices of its elders, and when Benedict was sent to Rome to complete his education he was revolted by the behaviour of his companions and decided to escape in order to avoid contamination. Accompanied by his old nurse, who had followed him to Rome to act as his housekeeper, he made his way to a village thirty miles from the capital. There in the peace of Enfide, he had time to consider his next step, realising that he was called by God to leave the world and enter upon the life of a solitary.

Travelling alone he penetrated further into wild, mountainous country. He made his home near Subiaco in a cave, so dangerous and difficult of access that for three years his presence there was unknown to any but a single monk from a neighbouring monastery. The monk, Romanus, supplied Benedict with a hair shirt and a monastic habit made from skins, and brought him bread which the anchorite drew up in a basket at the end of a rope.

Solitude did not free Benedict from the temptations of the flesh, and on one occasion he was so assailed by the memory of a woman he had formerly seen that he was on the point of leaving his cave. In desperation he stripped off his garments and rolled in a patch of briars until his whole body was torn and bleeding. 'Thus', says St Gregory, 'through those bodily wounds he cured the wounds of his soul.'

Benedict's life as a hermit ended when he was discovered by a priest who had heard a voice telling him that, while he prepared his dinner on Easter Sunday, Benedict, the servant of God, was fasting. After that he was visited by shepherds, who listened readily when he preached to them. His fame spread, and he was approached by the monks of a community at Vicovaro whose abbot had died asking him to be their ruler. He first refused but at last went with them. His rule proved more than they had bargained for, and they attempted to poison him. As Benedict made the sign of the cross over the jug of wine it broke in pieces. He returned thankfully to his cave, but not to the seclusion for which he longed.

Disciples of all descriptions flocked to him. He established twelve wooden-built monasteries, each with a complement of twelve monks and a prior. He ruled from his own establishment where he trained chosen monks himself. It was the beginning of the great monastic scheme which was to play a vital part in the regeneration of Western civilization.

When the monasteries at Subiaco were well established, the good name of the communities, and even the life of their founder, were threatened by the jealousy of a neighbouring priest, Florentius. He slandered St Benedict and attempted to poison him, and finally tried to demoralize the brethren so that Benedict withdrew to Monte Cassino, where paganism was still practised. The preaching and example of the great saint made many converts, and on the site of the former temple of Apollo whose idol he had overthrown, he built two chapels. To these other buildings were gradually added, and thus grew the home of the Benedictine order whose light was to dissipate the gloomy chaos of the dark ages.

St Benedict was abbot of Monte Cassino for fourteen years. His rule was severe but sensible. Extreme austerities were discouraged, and when a monk imposed penance upon himself by chaining his foot to a rock, he was smartly rebuked by a message from his superiors: 'If you are truly a servant of God, confine yourself not with a chain of iron, but with the chain of Christ.' Benedict's activities were extended far beyond his own monastery, he worked many miracles, he cured the sick, distributed alms to the poor, and in a time of famine once gave away almost all the food in the monastery. He was gifted with second sight, and one of his many prophesies which were fulfilled, was the destruction of the abbey by the Lombards, forty years later.

Totila the Goth visited Benedict, and was so awed by the majesty of his presence that he fell on his face before him. The Saint raised him from the ground and rebuked him for his cruelty, telling him that it was time that his iniquities should cease. He foretold, rightly, as the events proved, that Totila should cross the sea, that he should reign nine years, and die in the tenth. Totila asked Benedict to remember him in his prayers and departed, to exhibit from that time an astonishing clemency and chivalry in his treatment of conquered peoples.

About the year 550 Benedict foretold his own death, and six days before the end he ordered his monks to dig his grave beside that of his dearly loved sister, St Scholastica, who had died forty days earlier. As soon as this was done he fell ill. He received the last sacraments and died, standing in the chapel, with his arms extended to heaven.

SHORT VERSION (*St Benedict*)

When Benedict as a young man was sent to Rome to complete his education he was so horrified by the bad behaviour of the city that he fled and eventually made his home in an almost impenetrable cave near Subiaco. He remained there for some years, but gradually disciples flocked to him; so he established twelve wooden-built monasteries which he ruled from Subiaco. Gossip forced Benedict to leave for Monte Cassino, where paganism was still practised. The preaching and example of the great saint made many converts, and on the site of the former temple of Apollo whose idol he had overthrown, he built two chapels. To these gradually the buildings of a great monastery were added, the home of the Benedictine order whose light was to dissipate the gloomy chaos of the dark ages. Benedict died there around 550.

St Mary Magdalene 22 JULY

According to the Gospel of St John, Mary Magdalene was the first person to meet the risen Christ. She was one of a band of women, who accompanied our Lord and put their possessions at his disposal. She stood at the foot of the Cross with our Lady and Salome, Mary, the wife of Cleophas, and St John. After the Crucifixion she came to the tomb, before daybreak, and found that the stone had been removed from the entrance. She ran to tell Simon Peter and John, but they finding the tomb empty, returned to their own homes. Mary remained, weeping and so met Jesus. In the Middle Ages the Church identified Mary Magdalene with Mary of Bethany, and the woman who was a sinner anointed our Lord's feet with ointment. Today that view is not accepted by most scholars. It is believed in the Greek Church that Mary Magdalene followed St John to Ephesus, and died and was buried there.

St James the Apostle 25 JULY

St James the Great, so called to distinguish him from the younger apostle of the same name, was the son of Zebedee and Salome, and the brother of St John Evangelist. He was also cousin to our Lord. He was a fisherman, and with his brother, and his partners St Peter and St Andrew, left his fishing at the summons of Jesus.

Our Lord called James and John Boanerges, meaning 'Sons of Thunder', presumably on account of their fire and energy. They were both present at the raising of Jairus' daughter, at the Transfiguration, and in Gethsemane at the beginning of our Lord's passion. It is not known where James preached after the Ascension, but there is a tradition in Spain that he spread the Gospel there, and according to St Jerome he preached to dispersed Jewish communities.

About fourteen years after the Crucifixion he was arrested with Peter during the persecution of Herod Agrippa I, and was beheaded. Eusebius relates that the accuser of James was so moved by the constancy and courage which he showed at his trial that he became a Christian and was himself condemned to be beheaded. As they went together to the place of execution be begged forgiveness from James. After a little consideration, the apostle embraced him, and they died together.

St James was buried at Jerusalem, but the Spanish tradition claims that his remains were translated to Galicia, and later to Compostella where his shrine became a famous place of pilgrimage in the Middle Ages.

SHORT VERSION (*St James the Apostle*)
St James was a Galilean fisherman in partnership with his brother John, St Peter and St Andrew. Our Lord called James and John, Boanerges, meaning 'Sons of Thunder', presumably on account of their fire and energy. They were both present at the raising of Jairus' daughter, at the Transfiguration, and in Gethsemane at the beginning of our Lord's passion. It is not known where James preached after the Ascension, but there is a tradition in Spain that he spread the Gospel there, and according to St Jerome he preached to dispersed Jewish

communities. About fourteen years after the Crucifixion he was arrested with Peter during the persecution of Herod Agrippa I, and was beheaded. His relics are claimed to be in the Cathedral of Compostella in Spain and the shrine there has been an important place of pilgrimage since the Middle Ages.

St Anne

Mother of the Blessed Virgin Mary

St Anne was the mother of our Lady, but stories about her are derived from Apocryphal Gospels. She is said to have been married to Joachim. For a long time the couple were childless, and Joachim was publicly reproached for this by the high priest. He retired to the desert to fast and pray for a child, and remained there forty days. At the same time Anne mourned and lamented, and as she prayed an angel appeared to her and said, 'Anne, the Lord has heard your prayer, and you shall conceive and bear a child, who shall be spoken of in all the world.' At the same time an angel appeared to Joachim, and presently Mary was born to them. The cult of St Anne goes back at least to the sixth century and in the Middle Ages she was particularly popular in England.

William Wilberforce

Social Reformer, 1833

William Wilberforce was born at Hull, on St Bartholomew's day, 1759. His father was a very wealthy merchant and naturally hoped his son would follow him into the business. As soon as he was old enough, however, young Wilberforce stood for election as the Member of Parliament for his native town. He easily beat his two opponents and thus at the age of twenty-one, he began the life of a fashionable gentleman in London.

Four years later, Wilberforce was staying at Scarborough in Yorkshire. There he met his old schoolmate now a priest, Isaac Milner. William was making plans for a continental holiday and on an impulse he asked Milner to join the party. Wilberforce's mother and sister were included and as they travelled from place to place, they were in one carriage and Wilberforce and Milner in another. Just as they were about to leave Nice, Wilberforce noticed a copy of William Law's *A Serious Call to a Devout and Holy Life* among his companion's things.

'What is this like?' he asked as he flipped through the pages. 'It is one of the best books ever written,' was the reply. Then Milner suggested that they take it with them, and read it on the journey. Wilberforce agreed. That book, and long talks with Milner, began to change Wilberforce's life. He started to say his prayers again, and began two habits that were to last for the rest of his life; getting up early in the morning in order to spend as long as possible in prayer; and keeping Sunday apart for God. Some two years after his return from that eventful holiday, Wilberforce was invited to a meal by a group of men and women nick-named 'The Clapham Sect', who had been for some time gathering information and evidence prior to an attack on the slave trade.

The huge labour force needed to cultivate the plantations of North and South America or the Carribean was not readily available to the European colonists. Portuguese traders were probably the first to supply what the planters needed, transporting two hundred negroes from West Africa to Brazil. By the sixteenth century England had taken a hand in this lucrative business and by 1770 England's share of the 100,000 slaves exported annually from West Africa, was between 40,000 and 60,000.

Slaves were obtained in three main ways. Sometimes the slave ships would land a party of men and natives would be kidnapped; or slaves were bought from professional slave traders, very often Arabs; or slaves could be bought from a native chief. They might be his prisoners captured in a local war with another village; or sometimes, if the Chief was particularly anxious for money, or better still spirits, he would sell men of his own village.

The journey by boat to the West Indies or to the Americas might take as long as four weeks. Three hundred or more slaves would be tightly packed into small ships. Each one had just enough room to lie flat on his back. He was chained to his next door neighbour and fed as cheaply, and therefore as badly, as possible. As many as a quarter died on the journey.

During the dinner the conversation was soon brought round to slavery. One of the guests at least genuinely believed that negroes on the plantations were much happier than ever they had been in Africa. Others were concerned for the welfare of the West Indian colonists if slavery were abolished to say nothing of the prosperity of Liverpool. To these objections someone else replied, 'Rather let Liverpool and the West Indian Islands be swallowed up in the sea, than this monstrous system of iniquity be carried on!' 'We know your opinion is the same, Wilberforce,' said his host. 'I wish you would take this up in Parliament.'

There was absolute silence. Seven pairs of eyes looked expectantly at Wilberforce. He paused and then said, 'Gentlemen, I am quite prepared, with God's help, to take up this cause in the House of Commons, provided no more proper person can be found.'

One year later, in 1788, Wilberforce rose from his seat in Westminster. The House of Commons was full for the long debate on a motion to abolish the slave trade. Everyone leaned forward, anxious not to miss a single word from the young member for Hull. Wilberforce spoke for three and a half hours and delivered one of the finest speeches that had ever been heard in the Palace of Westminster. He concluded, 'Sir, when we think of eternity and of the future consequence of all human conduct, what is there in this life that shall make any man contradict the dictates of his conscience, the principles of justice and the laws of God.'

His eloquence was unavailing. Friends of the West Indian planters and other slave owners were naturally bitterly opposed to any tampering with the trade. The motion was defeated and although Wilberforce brought the question up annually, he had to wait eighteen years until 25 March 1806, before the Slave Trade was abolished.

That was only half the battle, once the capture and export of natives had been prohibited Wilberforce and his friends set about a campaign against slavery itself.

In 1833, within a mile of the Palace of Westminster where the House of Commons was discussing a Bill to abolish slavery, Wilberforce lay dying. He had been following the fortunes of the latest Bill with very eager attention. Parliament had accepted that if slaves in British Territory were to be freed, then Britain had to pay compensation to their owners. On 25 July the last problem had been settled and the Bill was ready to pass its final stages.

'When Mr Wilberforce hears of it,' said one of his friends, addressing the Commons, 'he may well exclaim, "Lord, now lettest thou thy servant depart in peace!"' A messenger was hastily dispatched with the wonderful news. 'Thank God', said the old man, as he listened to what had been agreed. 'Thank God, that I should have lived to witness a day in which England is willing to give £20,000,000 for the abolition of slavery.'

He died four days later, on 29 July 1833. Within a year and two days, on 31 July 1834, 800,000 slaves became free.

SHORT VERSION (*William Wilberforce*)
He entered Parliament as M.P. for Hull, the place of his birth, in 1780. He was twenty-one and his main concern was for his own advancement. Eight years later he was introducing the House of Commons to his first Bill to abolish slavery throughout the British Dominions. That Bill was rejected decisively but Wilberforce would not give in, and every year between 1788 to 1805 he introduced a similar motion. In 1806 the slave trade was abolished but it was not until 1833 that the slaves were finally

emancipated and by which time Wilberforce was dead. Wilberforce dated his conversion to a continental holiday he took not many years after he entered Parliament, during which he was greatly affected by William Law's *Serious Call*. Coupled with a direct request from his friends of the Clapham Sect this led him, despite much physical pain which he endured for most of his life, to take up in the name of God the cause of the abolition of slavery.

St Dominic

Priest, Friar, 1221

Dominic was the youngest of four children, three sons who spent their lives in the service of the Church, and a daughter whose two sons became preaching friars. He spent his early schooldays in the care of an uncle who was an archpriest, and at fourteen entered the University of Palencia. At twenty-five he was made a canon of Osma and for seven years shared the community life of the cathedral chapter under the rule of St Augustine. He was made at thirty-one, prior of the chapter, but shortly afterwards was removed from the contemplative life to one of active preaching in the world.

In the year 1204 the Bishop of Osma chose Dominic to accompany him on a mission to Denmark to negotiate a marriage between the son of Alfonso IX, King of Castile, and the daughter of the Danish king. On their journey they passed through Languedoc, the stronghold of the Albigensian heresy. They lodged at the house of an Albigensian, with whom Dominic spent the hours of darkness in discussion. By morning the man was converted from the heresy, and Dominic continued his journey with the bishop. But from that time he knew what his mission in life was to be.

The Albigensian heresy was a serious and growing threat to the Church, maintaining that all matter was evil. Its extreme forms often appealed to the common people, who were impressed by the abstinence and austerity of its followers. The Cistercians had been appointed by the pope to combat the heresy, but they had failed to stem the tide of fanaticism, and the weapon of persecution was proving useless. Dominic maintained that the heresy could be more effectively opposed by a preaching order whose members could show an example of living equal to that of their opponents, and who would rely on methods of clear instruction in the elements of the Catholic faith. 'Arm yourself with prayer, rather than a sword', he advised the Bishop of Toulouse, 'wear humility rather than fine clothes.'

Pope Innocent III consented to the establishment of the Dominican order of preachers, and its influence spread rapidly through Italy, Spain, France, Germany and Poland. Dominic founded convents for the shelter and instruction of converted women. The first community of Dominicans assembled at Toulouse and began common life in the friary which he built there.

On 6 August 1221, Dominic died at Bologna. A contemporary, Jordan of Saxony, wrote of him: 'Nothing disturbed the even temper of his soul except his quick sympathy with every sort of suffering. And as a man's face shows whether his heart is happy or not, it was easy to see from his friendly and joyous countenance that he was at peace inwardly.'

SHORT VERSION (*St Dominic*)

In 1204 the Bishop of Osma took a young Canon of his Cathedral with him on a journey to Denmark. The Bishop was to negotiate a Royal Marriage on behalf of his King, Alfonso IX of Castile. During their journey the Canon, Dominic, first met an Albigensian heretic and after an all night discussion restored him to the Church. The experience of this journey convinced Dominic of the need for an Order of Preachers whose members by their words and example would commend the faith to those who were following error. The influence of these Dominicans quickly spread throughout Europe though Dominic himself died in 1221.

St Oswald

5 AUGUST

King of Northumbria, 642

Oswald, described by Bede as a man beloved of God, succeeded his apostate brother Eanfrid as King of Bernicia. He defeated the heathen English King Cadwallada at Denisesburn in spite of Cadwallada's superior forces. Before giving battle Oswald erected a cross and summoned his army, crying: 'Let us all kneel together and ask the true and living God Almighty of his mercy to protect us from the arrogant savagery of our enemies, since he knows that we fight in just cause to save our nation.' For many years afterwards the place of his holy cross was revered as a source of miracles, and the brothers of the Abbey at Hexham built a church on the site.

The Scottish elders had baptised Oswald and his followers at the time of his exile, and after his victory over Cadwallada the king asked them to send him a bishop to establish the Christian faith in his kingdom. In response they sent him St Aidan, and King Oswald appointed the island of Lindisfarne as his see.

Bede tells how Oswald listened humbly and readily to Aidan's advice and diligently set himself to secure and extend the Church of Christ throughout his kingdom. In the early days of Aidan's ministry, before he could speak the English tongue fluently, the king himself would translate the word of God to his followers for the bishop. Priests and monks flocked over the border into Britain, preaching Christianity in all the provinces under Oswald's rule, while the king gave money and lands to establish monasteries.

Gradually the kingdom and provinces of Britain were united under Oswald. Humble, kind and generous, the king often prayed from the hour of the midnight office until day. He was accustomed to sit with his hands turned upwards on his knees, an attitude which had become habitual to him from constant prayer.

One Easter, as Oswald sat down to dine with St Aidan, the king's almoner announced the arrival of a number of paupers begging for alms. The king immediately ordered his own food to be distributed, and the silver dish broken in pieces and divided among them. Taking hold of the king's right hand

Aidan exclaimed: 'May this hand never perish.'

King Oswald was killed at Maserfield in the ninth year of his reign. He fell in battle against the heathen king of Mercia, and his last words were a prayer for the souls of his soldiers which became a proverb: 'O God, be merciful to their souls, as said Oswald as he fell.' He was dismembered and his head and limbs nailed to a tree. 'Oswald's tree' may have been the derivation of the Oswestry of today. Oswald was succeeded by his brother Oswin, who removed the saint's head for burial at Lindisfarne and the arms and body at Bamburgh.

SHORT VERSION (*St Oswald*)

When King Oswald of Northumbria wanted a bishop to lead a mission to his pagan subjects he naturally turned to Iona, who sent him St Aidan. Oswald gave Aidan the east coast of the island of Lindisfarne and from that base, king and bishop carried the Gospel throughout the area. Before Aidan had learned to speak to the people in their own tongue, Oswald acted as interpreter. Gradually the whole Kingdom was converted, but Oswald was killed in battle at Maserfield in 642.

St Laurence

10 AUGUST

Deacon, Martyr, 258

In 257 Valerian issued his first edict against Christians, and Pope Sixtus II and six of his deacons who were responsible among other things for the distribution of alms were martyred. Laurence, the seventh deacon, is said to have followed Sixtus to execution saying: 'Father, where are you going without your deacon?' Sixtus comforted him with the prophecy that within three days Laurence should follow him. In joyful preparation for his reunion with his master Laurence sought out all the poor dependants of the Church and divided among them all the money in his charge, even increasing the sum by the sale of sacred vessels. These transactions came to the notice of the prefect of Rome who ordered Laurence to render up the treasures of the Christian Church to the emperor within three days. Laurence employed these days in mustering the lame, the blind, widows, orphans and all other unfortunates who owed their preservation to Christian charity. On the third day he invited the prefect to inspect the treasure of the Church and confronted him with this assembly of want and misery. The prefect, enraged and disappointed, ordered that Laurence should be put to death by burning on a gridiron over a slow fire. Throughout his martyrdom the saint showed no sign of suffering, and witnesses said that his face was like that of an angel. St Augustine wrote that the martyr 'felt not the torments of the persecutor, so passionate was his desire of possessing Christ'. Once he spoke to his executioners and said: 'Turn me, I am done on this side.' He died praying that Rome might be converted and the faith of Christ spread then throughout the world.

St Clare of Assisi   11 AUGUST
Virgin, 1253

When she was eighteen, Clare heard Francis of Assisi preaching the Lenten sermon in her parish church of St George, and he fired her with a determination to follow Francis, especially in his pursuit of the 'Lady Poverty'. She fled from home on Palm Sunday 1212. At the Portiuncula, in the little chapel of St Mary of the Angels, Francis cut off her beautiful locks of hair and gave her a rough habit. The Franciscans had no nunnery, so Clare was taken to a Benedictine House from which her enraged family tried to tear her away but Clare clung to the altar. Soon others joined her, including her younger sister Agnes, and Francis found a home for them all at San Damiano. For forty years, long after the death of St Francis, Clare lived at San Damiano unable by reason of the conventions of the day to share the life of the Brothers but the Sisters lived a life of poverty and prayer.

Jeremy Taylor   13 AUGUST
Bishop of Down & Connor, Pastor, and Teacher, 1667

Jeremy's father was a barber in Cambridge and it was to that University that he went in 1626. He was ordained and his fame as a preacher albeit still a young man, came to the ears of Archbishop Laud who made him his chaplain. He became vicar of Uppingham but it was at the time of the Civil War and Jeremy supported King Charles to whom he became chaplain. He spent the first part of the Commonwealth quietly in Wales but in 1658 he accepted a teaching post in Ireland. At the Restoration Jeremy was appointed Bishop of Down and Connor, and he died there in 1667. Although he wrote and published a great deal, including treatises on the Real Presence and on Episcopacy, he is chiefly remembered for his two little books on the Christian life: *Holy Living* and *Holy Dying* both of which, but particularly the former, have continued as a source of inspiration for many Christians.

St Bernard

Abbot of Clairvaux, 1153

St Bernard was born in 1090 at Fontaines, a castle near Dijon belonging to his father, a Burgundian nobleman. He was the third son in a family of seven children. His brothers were educated as soldiers, but Bernard was sent to Chatillon to a college of secular canons. In childhood he was shy, thoughtful and fond of solitude, but he showed great aptitude for learning and seemed destined for a career as a scholar. One Christmas Eve as he waited to go to Matins with his mother he fell asleep and had a particularly vivid dream of the infant Christ in the stable at Bethlehem. This roused in him a special devotion to the mystery of the Incarnation which affected him for the rest of his life.

In his early manhood Bernard's talent, charm and goodness brought him success and popularity which might well have turned him from any serious consideration of the religious life, but gradually the world, with its bright prospect of learning and distinction, failed to satisfy him and he began to think of entering the monastery of Citeaux. Citeaux was then becoming notable for the severity of its rule, an off-shoot from the Benedictine. From this younger house the term Cistercian came into being. Bernard was still undecided when he entered a roadside church and prayed that God would guide him and make known his will. He rose from his knees with his doubts resolved, and in spite of all efforts to dissuade him he entered the monastery of Citeaux a few weeks later.

So great was Bernard's personal magnetism, even at the age of twenty-two, that he persuaded four of his brothers, an uncle and several friends to accompany him. Thirty-two men in all presented themselves that Easter for admission to a religious house of such austere rule that for several years the abbot, St Stephen Harding, had had no novices. Bernard desired only to die to the world and occupy himself with God for the rest of his mortal life, but after three years the Abbot ordered him to take twelve monks and found a new house at La Ferte, in the diocese of Langres. There the thirteen monks cleared land in the Valley of Wormwood, and with the help of the bishop and the country people built themselves a house. The first winter was one of almost unendurable hardship. They had no stores and lived chiefly on roots and bread made from such barley as they had been able to grow on poor land. Bernard imposed such severe discipline that his monks became discouraged, but later he discovered himself at fault in this and subjected himself to a long period of silence as a penance. The reputation of the monastery became so great that its numbers increased rapidly, and the name of the valley was changed to Clairvaux because it now lay in the eye of the sun.

After 1121 a great number of miracles were ascribed to Bernard, of which he said: 'I cannot think what these miracles mean, or why God has seen fit to work them through such a one as I. Signs and wonders have been wrought by holy men and by deceivers, I am not conscious of being either a holy man or a deceiver. I know that I have not those holy merits which are witnessed to by miracles.' He concluded that they were meant 'not to honour me but to admonish others.' During the next fifteen years, which he passed mainly at Clairvaux, his fame spread across Europe and his influence was felt through the voluminous correspondence which he kept up with all kinds of people. Multitudes wrote to him for advice, and any wrong which came to his knowledge drew a letter of rebuke from him. Among the persons of considerable importance who received such letters of remonstrance were the King of France and the Abbot of Cluny.

Ill health had caused Bernard to be dispensed from work in the fields, but he was ordered to undertake extra preaching duties. This led to the publication of his many treatises, the most important of which is one written for the guidance of Pope Eugenius III. Bernard reminds Eugenius that multiplicity of affairs may lead to forgetfulness of God and hardness of heart. He had described himself earlier as: 'over-run in all quarters with anxieties, suspicions, cares, and there is scarcely an hour that is left free from the crowd of discordant applicants, from the trouble and care of business. I have no power to stop their coming and cannot refuse to see them, and they do not leave me even the time to pray.'

For four years after 1130 Bernard was occupied in the disputes arising from a contested papal election. He supported the claim of Innocent II against the anti-pope Anacletus II and travelled throughout France, Germany and Italy pleading his cause. It was from one of these journeys that he had returned with Peter Bernard of Paganelli as a postulant, and the future Pope Eugenius III was put to stoke the monastery fires.

Politically and spiritually Bernard had become the most influential man in Europe. After the settlement of the papal schism he came into relentless conflict with Peter Abelard, the greatest scholar of his time. Bernard was impelled in his savage persecution of Abelard by his sense of the dangers of excessive rationalism and the arrogant exaltation of reason above faith. In spite of all these claims upon his time from the world, Bernard continued to preach to his monks, and Clairvaux became the mother-house of sixty-eight monasteries, including Rievaulx and Fountains in England, and Mellifont in Ireland, under its abbot St Malachy.

In 1153 Bernard undertook his last journey, a successful mission to reconcile the quarrelling province of Metz and Lorraine. He persuaded them to settle their differences and accept the treaty which he drew up. His health had been failing for some time and he returned to Clairvaux to meet the death for which he longed. When his monks implored him to stay with them he cried, 'I am straitened between two and what to chose I know not. I leave it to the Lord; let Him decide.'

SHORT VERSION (*St Bernard of Clairvaux*)

Bernard was born of wealthy parents at their castle near Dijon in 1090. He proved to be a very clever lad, and also very persuasive, for when he was twenty-two he encouraged four of his brothers and an uncle to enter the recently founded Cistercian Abbey of Citeaux with him. Three years later he was ordered by the Abbot to take twelve monks and found a new monastery at La Ferte. This was to remain Bernard's home for the rest of his life though it was renamed Clairvaux after the monks had cleared the forest and so let the light of the sun into the valley. Bernard's influence spread far beyond his abbey and kings were among his correspondents. He tried to mediate in the squabbles of the Church, preached regularly both to his monks and to others, and wrote books and biblical commentaries which are still read today. Bernard died at Clairvaux in 1153.

St Bartholomew the Apostle

Beyond the fact of his existence little is known of St Bartholomew. Scholars of later date than those of the early Church identify him with Nathanael of Cana in Galilee. He is also counted among the Apostles to whom Christ appeared after the Resurrection, standing unrecognised on the shore of the sea of Tiberias. According to legend Bartholomew carried the Gospel to India. St Pantaenus, a Christian philosopher of Alexandria, found in India some traces of Christianity and was shown a copy of St Matthew's Gospel in Hebrew which he was told had been brought there by Bartholomew. Later Armenian writers held that St Bartholomew was martyred by flaying and beheading at Albanopolis (Derbend, on the Caspian Sea) after conducting his mission in Greater Armenia. Earlier Armenian writers barely mention him.

St Augustine
28 AUGUST

Bishop of Hippo, Teacher of the Faith, 430

St Augustine, Aurelius Augustine, the greatest Father and Doctor of the Latin Church, was born on 13 November 354, at Tagaste, a small village in Numidia. His father, Patricius, was a pagan for the greater part of his life; but Augustine was instructed in the Christian faith by his mother, Monica, to such effect that, in spite of the intellectual curiosity which attracted him to pagan philosophies, he was never able to break completely away from what he later recognised as the inescapable truth of the Bible. He wrote at last of himself as 'sealed with the mark of Christ's cross and salted with his salt'.

Idle, intelligent, sensual and rebellious, his early education was distracted by these qualities, but he was intensely aware of the mystery of life, and at the age of seventeen he was sent to Carthage where he distinguished himself in the study of rhetoric. He read the Neo-Platonic writings and was profoundly influenced by Cicero's *Hortensius*, an exhortation to philosophy which altered his affections and completely changed his purpose in life. Henceforward he was to seek after truth, but it was to be a long time before he found it. During his student years at Carthage Augustine's father died, and he himself became the father of a son, Adeolatus. By the age of twenty he had mastered most of the liberal sciences as they were then understood and had allied himself with the Manichees, a sect composed of the followers of a Persian religion. Although he abandoned Manichaeism later it permanently affected his religious conceptions.

Returning to Tagaste he opened a school of rhetoric there, but the year 380 found him again at Carthage where he settled for another three years. There, at the age of twenty-six, he wrote *The Beautiful and the Fitting*, the fruit of his studies in aesthetics. In the year 383 Augustine journeyed to Rome as a teacher of rhetoric. He joined the Academicians but found no satisfaction in their conflict of philosophies, and he abandoned Manichaeism, disillusioned by its despairing and negative attitudes and lack of ethical code. From Rome he proceeded to Milan and under the influence of the Bishop of Milan, St

Ambrose, he studied the Epistles of St Paul and was irrevocably converted to Christianity.

At Milan St Augustine was joined by his mother, and at Monica's insistence he parted for ever with Lucilla, the mother of his bastard son Adeolatus. His mistress returned to Africa, and in 386 he resigned his lectureship and retired with his mother, his son and his friend Alypius to Cassiacum to prepare for baptism. Adeolatus, who was then in his fifteenth year, died shortly afterwards. Inspired by an African, Pontitian, who drew Augustine's attention to the lives of St Anthony and the desert hermits, he resolved to return to Africa to form a religious household. On the journey Monica died at Ostia, and after pausing at Rome for a while Augustine arrived in Africa in the year 388. Selling his estate and distributing the proceeds to charity, Augustine formed a small monastic establishment where he lived as a recluse. Three years later he was summoned by Valerius, the aged Greek Bishop of Hippo, to accept ordination and to act as his mouthpiece to the Latin-speaking community. Four years after his ordination Valerius consecrated him Colleague Bishop, and Augustine until his death in 430 preached and worked indefatigably in the diocese. Probably no other theologian has exercised so profound an influence on the development of Christian doctrine.

SHORT VERSION (*St Augustine of Hippo*)
Augustine had left his friends in another part of the garden. Suddenly in the stillness he heard a child's voice crying, 'Take up and read.' Quickly Augustine returned to his friends and looked at the book of Paul's letters open at Romans. His eyes focused on, 'Put on the Lord Jesus Christ, and make no provision for the flesh to gratify its desires.' It was enough. The long prayer of St Monica, Augustine's mother, were answered and he believed. Augustine was 32 and over the next forty-four years became one of the foremost theologians within the Church. In 395 he was consecrated bishop and succeeded as Bishop of Hippo in North Africa, where he remained until his death in 430. It seems likely that no other single writer has had such an effect on Western theology as Augustine, while both his *Confessions* and *City of God* to name the most famous of his books are still being constantly reprinted.

112

St Aidan

Bishop of Lindisfarne, Missionary, 651

St Aidan was sent from his monastery on Iona to be bishop of Northumbria in response to a request from King Oswald for someone to lead a mission to his people. According to Bede, Oswald recognised in Aidan a man of outstanding gentleness, holiness and moderation and gave him the island of Lindisfarne, or Holy Isle. Lindisfarne, which is joined to the mainland twice a day at low tide, lies off the Northumbrian coast between Berwick and Bamburgh, stretching a long finger of basaltic rock towards the mouth of the Tweed. On this small, bleak island, Aidan founded his episcopal monastery under the rule of St Columcille, so that it became the religious capital of Northern England and Southern Scotland, and the residence of the first sixteen bishops of Northumbria, including St Cuthbert.

Under the active protection of Oswald and his successor Oswin, Christianity spread rapidly through Northumbria. Other monks followed Aidan to assist in his apostolate. Bede writes that Aidan showed all the evidences of holy life, and the highest recommendation of his teaching to all was that he and his followers lived as they taught, neither seeking nor caring for wordly possessions. 'So free were they from avarice that no one would receive lands or possessions for building monasteries unless compelled to by the secular power.' Aidan, where possible, reserved for himself only, a site for a chapel with a chamber attached where he could write his sermons. He cultivated peace and love, purity and humility; he was above anger and greed, and despised pride and conceit. 'He used his priestly authority to check the proud and powerful . . . he relieved and protected the poor.'

The monastery of Lindisfarne undertook in perpetuity the education of twelve English boys to be brought up to the service of Christ. Every church and monastery became a school, and St Aidan worked indefatigably for the welfare of slaves, many of whom were ransomed with the alms bestowed on the Church. Several miracles are recorded of St Aidan, among them that of the raising of the siege of the royal city of

Bamburgh. The forces of Penda set fire to brushwood piled against the walls, but the prayers of St Aidan caused the wind to change direction, and the flames and smoke rolled back upon the invaders 'so injuring and unnerving them that they abandoned their assault on a city so clearly under God's protection'.

Aidan died 31 August 651 twelve days after the murder of his patron King Oswy, under a tent erected against the wall of his church near Bamburgh which he was using as a centre for the mission which had brought him there.

SHORT VERSION (*St Aidan*)

St Aidan was sent from Iona to be Bishop of Northumbria in response to a request from King Oswald for someone to lead a mission to his people. Aidan settled in the island of Lindisfarne which twice a day at low tide is joined to the Northumbrian mainland by a causeway. There Aidan built his monastery which also became a school as well, and from there, often accompanied by King Oswald himself, the godly bishop set out on his missionary journeys to the people of the North. In 642 Aidan was at least able to ensure that the head of his friend King Oswald was given Christian burial at Bamburgh. He himself lived a further nine years, dying in 651. He was buried on Lindisfarne but the Abbey is now in ruins.

John Bunyan

Author, 1688

John Bunyan came from a very old Bedfordshire family, and he was fourteen years old when the Civil War broke out. In 1644 he was called up for the army of Parliament, but does not appear to have been involved in any battles. He was released three years later, returned to his trade as a tinker, and married in 1649. During this time he had been developing greater and greater sympathies with the Puritans and in 1653 he was baptised in the River Ouse by Pastor John Gifford. Two years after that he preached his first sermon. When Charles II returned and an attempt was made to enforce religious conformity by law, John was arrested for preaching without a licence and for refusing to attend his parish church. He was gaoled and not released until 1666 whereupon he resumed his preaching and was promptly gaoled again until 1672. A short respite was followed by a fourth period of imprisonment and he died in London in 1688. It was while he was in Bedford prison that he wrote the book *The Pilgrim's Progress* which next to the Bible, has had the greatest influence in the formation of the English nation. It is in fact only one of a large number of books that he published, but few others are now remembered.

St Gregory the Great 3 SEPTEMBER
Bishop of Rome, Teacher of the Faith, 604

St Gregory was the first monk to become pope. When he was elected to the papacy, Rome was almost in ruins after the years of war between Justinian and the Ostrogoths, which had ended in victory for Justinian. Gregory was educated for a legal career, and by the time he was thirty he was prefect, the highest civil office in Rome. With money left to him by his father he had founded six Benedictine monasteries in Sicily before he turned his own house into a monastery dedicated to St Andrew. To that he retired as a novice, spending several years there, and practising austerities so severe that his health was permanently injured.

After these years of seclusion, which he counted the happiest of his life, Gregory was ordained seventh deacon of the Roman Church and sent as papal ambassador to the magnificent Byzantine court at Constantinople. On his return to Rome he was abbot of his monastery. It may have been about this time that Gregory noticed three golden-haired, fair-skinned boys for sale in the market, and enquired their nationality. Bede tells the traditional story: 'They are Angles or Anglii' was the reply. 'They are well-named', said the saint, 'for they have angelic faces and it becomes such to be companions with the angels in heaven.' Learning that they were pagans, he asked what province they came from, and was told that they had been brought from Deira. 'De ira!' exclaimed Gregory; 'Yes, verily they shall be saved from God's ire and called to the mercy of Christ. What is the name of the king of that country?' 'Aella.' 'Then must Alleluia be sung in Aella's land.' He hastened to the Pope and obtained leave to go the Britain as a missionary, but before he had gone three days on his journey he was recalled at the demand of the populace. Whatever modern historians may think of this tradition, there is no doubt that St Gregory sent St Augustine to England in 596 and supported his mission with supplies of books, relics, vestments and reinforcements of missionaries.

At the death of Pelagius II, Gregory was unanimously chosen to succeed him, although he had no wish to become Pope.

During a severe outbreak of the plague in Rome he ordered a processional litany through the city. The procession traversed the streets for three days chanting 'Kyrie eleison', and the pestilence quickly diminished and ceased. At the end of the processions an angel was said to have appeared on the summit of Hadrian's mausoleum, sheathing his sword in token that the plague was stayed.

As Pope his industry was remarkable. He was a most painstaking administrator, 'ruling prudently with all his power', as numerous letters which survive bear witness. Besides the work of administration he preached and wrote books—and his well-known *Dialogues*. He is credited with the revision of the system of church music, and the composition of several great hymns. After his death he was criticised for his depletion of the Church's money, but his vast charities must have saved hundreds of poor people from starvation in a period of severe distress. He allowed no oppression of the Jews and would not permit them to be deprived of their synagogues, declaring that they must be converted by charity.

All this was accomplished in spite of chronic ill-health. He wrote to a friend towards the end of his life: 'I have been unable to rise from my bed. I am tormented by the pains of gout; a kind of fire seems to pervade my whole body; to live is pain. I look forward to death as the only remedy.' He died on 11 March 604.

SHORT VERSION (*St Gregory*)

It is said of Gregory that he once saw three blond fair-skinned boys up for sale in Rome's slave market. When he asked what tribe they came from he was told they were Angles from England. 'Not Angles but angels' replied Gregory and he decided to obtain papal approval for a mission to England. He was too late. The Pope died and despite his protests Gregory was elected to succeed him. Unable to go to England he sent Augustine. Gregory, the first monk to become Pope, proved an able administrator. He preached and wrote books, among them a book on the duties of bishops. He is credited with the revision of the system of church music, and the composition of several great hymns. After his death he was criticised for his depletion of the Church's money, but his vast charities must have saved hundreds of poor people from starvation in a period of severe distress. He allowed no oppression of the Jews and would not permit them to be deprived of their synagogues, declaring that they must be converted by charity. He died on 11 March 604.

St Cyprian

13 SEPTEMBER

Bishop of Carthage, Martyr, 258

St Cyprian was born about the year 200, probably at Carthage. Of his life before conversion little is known, except that he was an orator, a barrister, and a notable figure, politically and socially, in that city. He was past middle age when he was converted by an elderly priest, Caecilian. Before baptism he made a vow of chastity. He applied himself to the study of Christian literature, and every day read the works of Tertullian. When he wanted them he would demand, 'Reach hither my master.' He was ordained priest, and in 248 was designated for the bishopric of Carthage. He sought to evade the office, some people opposed his election, but in the end he gave way and was consecrated.

After a year of Cyprian's excellent rule as bishop, the Emperor Decius commenced a persecution of Christians. In the years of peace and tolerance the Christian community had grown slack; many had been admitted whose faith was not likely to withstand any severe test, and apostates flocked to register their return to paganism. Cyprian was proscribed and his property declared forfeit. He withdrew into hiding, earning a great deal of criticism. He defended his action in letters to the clergy, and lived to see his policy justified, since the Church at that time needed guidance and encouragement more than it needed martyrs.

After fifteen months the persecution diminished and Cyprian returned to face new problems. A schismatic priest, Novatus, was receiving returned apostates into full communion without canonical penance. Cyprian condemned the practice and Novatus hurried to Rome to enlist the approval of Novatian, the anti-pope who stood in opposition to Pope Cornelius. Cyprian supported Cornelius, and with St Dionysius, Bishop of Alexandria, obtained the collaboration of the eastern bishops. His treatise *On Unity* is still a classic exposition of the divine foundation of the episcopate, descending in direct succession from the Apostles.

In 253 peace was restored to the Church, but plague broke out in Carthage. Cyprian's sympathy for the needy and suffering showed itself in his organisation of relief, and his insistence that friends, enemies and persecutors should be succoured alike without discrimination.

The plague was followed by a second persecution in 257 under Valerian and Gallienus. Cyprian was banished for a year, during which he directed his see and wrote copiously. He produced a treatise on the invalidity of heretical baptism, a subject on which he had fallen out with the Roman Church, expressing his opinion with more warmth than was considered becoming in a bishop. His stringent views on the matter were never accepted.

In 258 an edict ordered the execution of all Christian bishops, priests and deacons. Cyprian made no attempt to escape. He was arrested and taken to Carthage where a vast crowd, pagan and Christian, gathered to do him honour. The next day he was brought before the proconsul, Galerius, who began a pompous cross examination. Cyprian cut him short. 'Do what you are ordered to do,' he said. 'In so simple a matter there is nothing to consider.'

Galerius sentenced him to death, which Cyprian acknowledged by saying, 'Thanks be to God.'

A great crowd followed him when he was led out to the plain of Sextus, the place of execution. Cyprian took off his cloak and bowed himself in prayer. Then he removed his dalmatic and waited for death in his white linen alb. He ordered his friends to give the executioner twenty-five pieces of gold, and then bandaged his eyes himself, the priest and the subdeacon tying the ends for him. The executioner trembled so that he could not perform his task, and the centurian took the sword and beheaded the saint with one stroke. All that day crowds came to view the body; at night it was removed by the Christians and buried by torch-light.

SHORT VERSION (*St Cyprian*)

Cyprian, probably born at Carthage, became somewhat reluctantly bishop of that city in 248, not so many years after his baptism. Before his conversion he was a lawyer and this background stood him in good stead as bishop. During the persecution of the Emperor Decius Cyprian hid, but afterwards became involved in the controversy over how apostates should be received back into the Church. Out of it came his book about the episcopate. In the course of a second persecution of Christians, Cyprian was beheaded in the year AD 258.

Saints and Martyrs of Australia and the Pacific

This commemoration could include:

New Guinea Martyrs, *1942*

During the occupation of New Guinea by the Japanese during World War Two the Church came in for a fair share of persecution. Among those who died there were two Englishmen, Vivian Redlich and John Barge, seven from Australia including Margery Brenchley, May Hayman and Mavis Parkinson, and Leslie Gariadi and Lucian Tapiedi, two Papuan evangelists.

James Chalmers, Oliver Tomkins and their companion Martyrs, *1901*

Chalmers and Tomkins, one an older man, Tomkins still in his twenties, were working in New Guinea for the London Missionary Society, and both were killed when they tried to break new ground in the Fly River district.

John Coleridge Patteson, Bishop of Melanesia, *Martyr, 1871*

Unlike many of the early missionaries, Patteson, an Englishman, made it a rule that, wherever possible, local customs of the islanders were not to be disturbed. He wanted to be their pastor, not their overlord, and he travelled among them constantly. On 21 September 1871 he landed on the island of Nukapu. He was attacked and killed, and his body launched on a canoe which drifted back to the ship. On his breast were five wounds, one for each islander who had been earlier slaughtered by white traders.

St Matthew the Apostle

St Matthew was a Jew, probably a Galilean. As a tax-gatherer for the Romans he belonged to a calling which barred him from sharing in the religious worship of the Jews, and set him apart in a class disliked and suspected by Gentiles as much as Jews. St Mark speaks of him as Levi. It is probable that the name of Matthew (gift of Jehovah) was bestowed on him after his call, in the second year of our Lord's ministry. According to Eusebius Matthew wrote his gospel in Aramaic to record the story of his master's earthly life and work for the benefit of his Jewish converts after he should have left them to preach to other nations. He is said to have preached in Ethiopia, and to have been the guest at one time of the eunuch of Queen Candace, and to have been slain with a sword in that country. More trustworthy traditions report him to have died a natural death, but he is generally venerated as a martyr.

Launcelot Andrewes 25 SEPTEMBER
Bishop of Winchester, 1626

Before he died Andrewes is said to have been able to read twenty-one languages, apart from his own, and of these, Latin, Greek and Hebrew he had acquired before he left school at sixteen. His whole life was essentially that of a scholar and woe betide any man who before midday interrupted him at his studies. At Cambridge his theological views tended to lie with the Puritans and it is suggested by some that he provided the first theological base for sabbatarianism, though his version was never extreme.

He was ordained while teaching at the university but left it in 1586 to become chaplain to the President of the Council of the North. He began there discussions with Roman Catholics in attempts to convince them that they were wrong. Later, when he was Bishop of Chichester, at the command of King James I, he entered the lists of controversy against Cardinal Bellermine, and later Cardinal Perron. In the course of the various charges and counter-charges, Andrewes, to quote a recent biographer 'was defining in a new way, where the Church of England stood both historically and theologically.' In 1601 Andrewes was appointed Dean of Westminster, and when King James authorised a new translation of the Bible, Andrewes became chairman of one of the six companies of scholars, charged with the work. His group was responsible for Genesis to 2 Kings inclusive, and it is obvious that much of that section came from Andrewes' own pen.

Launcelot Andrewes was consecrated Bishop of Chichester in 1605, translated to Ely four years later, and in spring 1619 moved to Winchester, whose Bishop he became six month's or more earlier. As bishop he was responsible for what was probably the first consecration of a new Church building after the Reformation, and modern rites of consecration of churches throughout the Anglican Communion owe much to him. He was also responsible for the general outlines of Anglican inductions. Andrewes preached frequently before the court, and King James admired and feared him, for the Bishop would not countenance any loose living either by courtier or the King himself. Nevertheless it was Andrewes who was summoned to James' death-bed.

Andrewes saw the coronation of Charles I but was dead by the end of the year. Of him it was once said that he was 'Doctor Andrewes' in the schools, 'Bishop Andrewes' in the pulpit, but in his chamber 'Saint Andrewes'. He used to spend four or five hours at prayer each day, and the selection of his *Private Prayers* that he gave to Archbishop Laud are a spiritual masterpiece.

SHORT VERSION (*Launcelot Andrewes*)

It was said of him that he was 'Doctor Andrewes' in the schools, 'Bishop Andrewes' in the pulpit, but in his chamber 'Saint Andrewes'. He used to spend many hours each day in prayer, and the selection of his *Private Prayers* which he gave to Archbishop Laud are a spiritual classic. He was Bishop of Chichester in 1605, went on to Ely in 1609 and finally moved to Winchester in 1619. His scholarship was breathtaking and he was one of the translators of the Authorised Version of the Bible. An ardent supporter of the Anglican position, he defined in a new way where that Church stands historically and theologically. His sermons would never do for the twentieth century, but King James I both admired and feared him, for the Bishop would not countenance loose living of any kind.

St Vincent de Paul   27 SEPTEMBER
Founder of the Vincentian Order, 1660

St Vincent de Paul was a Gascon, born at Pouy, near Bayonne. His father was a peasant farmer, and Vincent was the third child in a family of four sons and two daughters. His intelligence and his inclination towards the priesthood showed in early life, and his father sent him to be educated by the Franciscan brethren at Dax, near his home. He later studied at Toulouse and was ordained at the age of twenty. He went to Paris and was appointed as one of the chaplains of Margaret de Valois.

In Paris Monsieur Vincent encountered a priest, Peter de Bérulle, afterwards Cardinal Bérulle, on whom he made a great impression. Up till this time he seems to have conformed to the extremely casual piety of the period, and to have had no particular aim other than preferment, but he had behaved with dignity, patience and restraint under the provocation of a false accusation which, after six months, was disproved. Peter Bérulle persuaded him to take a post as chaplain and tutor in the household of Philip de Gondi, Count of Joigny.

In 1617, during a visit with the de Gondis to their estate, the neglect of the peasantry was brought to Monsieur Vincent's notice. A peasant, who believed himself to be dying, confessed to him that his previous confessions had been invalid, and therefore sacrilegious. With the wholehearted approval of Madame de Gondi, Monsieur Vincent began to preach in the church at Folleville. His sermons on confession and repentance soon drew such crowds of penitents that he had to call upon the Jesuits to assist him.

The same year, at the instigation of Father de Bérulle, Vincent became pastor of Chatillon-les-Dombes. He extended his work of reformation to embrace all classes, and many notable sinners were moved by his preaching to amend their scandalous lives. Returning to Paris he commenced his famous work among the galley slaves imprisoned in the Conciergerie.

The de Gondi family offered to endow a perpetual mission to the common people to be conducted entirely under the direction of Monsieur Vincent. His diffidence caused him to refuse, but later their inspiration bore fruit in the foundation of a community of missioners who were to renounce ecclesiastical preferment and work among the small towns and villages. St Vincent never forgot his peasant origin, he loved the working people for their patience and endurance. But he did not despise the rich. He gathered them, men and women, into his Confraternity of Charity, and set them to work at visiting hospitals and the homes of the poor.

At the death of his patroness, Monsieur Vincent joined the new community in the College des Bons Enfants which the Archbishop of Paris had made over to them. In 1633 they were presented with the priory of Saint Lazare which was to be their chief house.

Vincent found that the preparation of candidates for priesthood was neglected. He established retreats for ordinands which were held at St Lazare, at first four times a year, and then six times. They each lasted a fortnight, and seventy to ninety ordinands were present at each. He followed this success by instituting retreats for laymen of all descriptions, and called St Lazare his Noah's Ark, because all sorts of animals were lodged there. 'This house', he said, 'was formerly used as a retreat for lepers; they were received here, and not one was cured. Now it is used to receive sinners, who are sick men covered with spiritual leprosy, but are cured by the grace of God; rather, they are dead men brought back to life. What joy to think that the house of St Lazare is a house of resurrection! Lazarus, after he had been three days in the tomb, came out alive, and our Lord who raised him up still gives the same grace to many who, after staying here some days as in the grave of Lazarus, come out of it with a new life.'

Allied to his Confraternity of Charity were the Sisters of Charity, whose 'convent is the sick-room, their chapel the parish church, their cloister the streets of the city'. Rich women were enlisted as Ladies of Charity to collect funds and work for causes of compassion. Hundreds of babies were abandoned in Paris every year. Once Vincent saw a man mutilating a baby for begging purposes. Moved with pity he established a Foundling Hospital, and night after night he is said to have wandered about the slums of Paris, bringing back to the hospital these deserted babies wrapped up in his cloak.

His influence at Court was great, even in political matters.

He was appointed to a Council of Conscience formed at his instigation to exercise a much-needed check on ecclesiastical appointments; at that time spiritual qualifications were hardly even considered. A lady of the court, infuriated at his refusal to recommend her son for a bishopric, flung a footstool at Monsieur Vincent. He left the room with blood pouring from his forehead, and said to a companion who waited for him, 'See to what length a mother's love for her son will go.' He died on 27 September 1660.

SHORT VERSION (*St Vincent de Paul*)

St Vincent de Paul was born of peasant stock in Gascony in 1576 and was ordained when he was only twenty. In the early years of his ministry he was not a particularly fervent Christian, but was certainly an ambitious man. All this changed when he came into contact first with a priest, later Cardinal, Peter de Bérulle, and second with the poor, and it is as a friend of the poor that he is chiefly remembered. He worked among the galley slaves imprisoned in Paris, and according to some, took the place of one of them for a time. He founded communities and confraternities of both men and women dedicated to serving the poor. To his sisters he said that their convent was the sick-room, their chapel the parish church and their cloister the street of the city. Vincent never spared himself and died worn out in 1660.

St Francis of Assisi   4 OCTOBER
Friar, 1226

St Francis was born at Assisi, in Umbria, about the year 1182. His father, Peter Bernadone, was a merchant, and his mother was of Provençal extraction. The family was wealthy, honourable and respected and Peter Bernadone spent much of his time in France in the course of business. At the birth of his son he was absent from home, and in allusion to this circumstance the child, who was christened John, was afterwards known as Francesco—the Frenchman. As a young man Francis was extravagant, generous, idle and well-behaved. Learning and commerce held no attractions for him, but his imagination was fired by the songs and legends of chivalry. When fighting broke out between the cities of Perugia and Assisi, he was taken prisoner and confined for a year. On his return he was seized with a serious illness, which he endured, as he had endured his imprisonment, with patience and cheerfulness. When he recovered he set out to join the army of Walter de Brienne in Southern Italy. Again he was taken ill, and this time he realised that his call to fight and serve must take a very different direction.

Francis returned to Assisi, and began his battle to mortify his own desires, by serving the sick and giving away his possessions. One day, as he prayed in the church of St Damiano, outside the walls of the town, he heard a voice saying, 'Francis, go and repair my house, which you see is falling down.' The command was repeated twice. To the grief and anger of his parents, he disinherited himself, and went forth wearing a ragged garment begged from a servant, on which he had inscribed a cross with chalk.

Francis spent two years in wandering through Italy, finding shelter in monasteries in return for work, sleeping rough at other times, begging, and always singing the praises of God. He returned to Assisi and set himself to repair the church of St Damiano. Many of his former associates thought him mentally deranged, others looked on his doings with sardonic amusement. Francis, as he begged and gathered subscriptions for the work, would say: 'Help me to finish this building. Here will one day be a monastery of nuns by whose good fame our

Lord will be glorified over the whole Church.' This prophecy was to be fulfilled within six years. When he was not raising funds he was carrying stones and acting as a builder's labourer.

He repaired an old church dedicated to St Peter, and after that a ruinous chapel belonging to the Benedictine monks of Monte Subasio. It was called Portiuncula (Little Portion) and was dedicated to our Lady of the Angels. On the feast of St Matthew, Francis attended Mass in the chapel of Our Lady of the Angels. The gospel for the day seemed to apply directly to himself, and he knew with complete certainty the way he must take: 'And as you go proclaim the message: "The kingdom of Heaven is upon you." Heal the sick, raise the dead, cleanse lepers, cast out devils. You received without cost; give without charge. Provide no gold, silver, or copper to fill your purse, no pack for the road, no second coat, no shoes, no stick; the worker earns his keep.' (Matt. 10.7–10).

One of the first disciples of St Francis was Bernard da Quintavalle, a rich gentleman of Assisi. He had invited Francis to spend a night at his house and overheard him at prayer, repeating over and over again the words, *Deus meus et Omnia*— 'My God and my all.' The next morning Bernard went to him and said, 'Brother, I am quite purposed in my heart to quit the world and follow you in whatever you tell me.'

After Bernard came Giles, and gradually a band of followers grew up about St Francis. He drew up a rule and it was informally approved in 1210 by Innocent III. The Pope was at first unwilling to countenance a new order when so many of the established orders were in need of reform, but he tonsured Francis and his disciples and gave them a commission to preach.

Francis, in his humility, would never aspire to the priesthood, preferring to remain a deacon. He called his order the Friars Minor. At first they lived in a small house outside the walls of Assisi, but as their numbers grew they built themselves huts of wood and clay. They wore the grey tunics of Italian peasants, tied about the waist with a rough cord. In twos and threes they wandered about the countryside, sleeping in hay-lofts or in the open, preaching, ministering to the sick and to lepers, begging their food and mixing with their fellow men. They worked as servants and labourers in return for food, being forbidden to accept money.

Their most distinctive mark was their gaiety. If asked to what order they belonged, they replied, 'We are penitents of Assisi.' Gloom and depression Francis thought akin to sin. 'It does not become a servant of God before his brother or anyone else to be sad, or have a troubled countenance. It belongs to the devil to be sad.' The rule of the Friars Minor was founded on three texts: 'If you would be perfect, go and sell what you have, and give to the poor.' 'Take nothing for your journey.' 'If any man wants to come after me, let him deny himself, and take up his cross and follow me.'

Communities of Friars sprang up throughout Italy in response to a universal demand, and within a few years missions were sent to other countries. The chapel at Portiuncula was handed over to St Francis in 1212 by the abbot of the Benedictine monastery. He made a condition that it should always remain the head church of the order. It is now enclosed within the church of Santa Maria degli Angeli.

With the growth of the order, it was inevitable that the original simplicity of its conception should be modified. St Francis strove to resist those who demanded a more practical organisation, and were, in his view, disposed to take far more thought for the morrow than was consistent with perfect trust in God. He said: 'The Lord has called me by the way of simplicity and humility, and this is the way he has pointed out to me for myself and for those who will believe and follow me ... The Lord told me that he would have me poor and foolish in this world, and that he willed not to lead us by any way other than by that. May God confound you by your own wisdom and learning and, for all your fault-finding, send you back to your vocation whether you will or no.' He protested against the admission of learned brethren to the end, partly because he seems to have had reason to distrust the effect of learning on life, but more because he felt that there was no room for a student class in the Order.

In 1219 Francis went to the East, and is said to have visited the camp of both Crusaders and the Saracens of Egypt. A contemporary account of him by a Crusader has come down: 'He is so lovable that he is venerated by every one. Having come into our army, he had not been afraid in his zeal for the faith to go to that of our enemies. For days together he announced the word of God to the Saracens, but with little success.'

Afterwards he visited the Holy Land, and obtained special permission from the sultan to see the Holy Sepulchre. On his return he found that certain innovations had been introduced into the Order, bringing it closer to the old-established monastic foundations. Cardinal Ugolini, a friend and patron, and the Roman Court, urged these changes. Francis seems to have consented against his better judgement, and in September 1220, he resigned the office of Superior. His last years were spent in protest. 'Almost everything that was done in the Order after 1221 was done without his knowledge or against his wish.'

Like so many other saints he had a great power over animals. Once he preached to the birds. His sermon began: 'My little sisters the birds, you owe much to God, your Creator, and always in every place ought you to praise him because he has given you liberty to fly about everywhere.' While he spoke, 'these birds began all of them to open their beaks and stretch their necks and spread their wings and bend their heads close to the ground'. When he rescued a hare from a trap it ran to him, and he said, 'Come to me, brother hare,' and took it in his arms and caressed it, and when he put it down, it would not run away, but kept returning. When a fisherman who was rowing him over a lake presented him with a large fish, he accepted the gift and put it back in the water, bidding it bless God.

In the August of 1224 Francis retired to a lonely mountain spot among the Appenines called La Verna, for forty days' fast and prayer before Michaelmas. On his way, while they rested under a tree, some small birds settled on his head and shoulders, and round his feet, and showed their delight by singing and flapping their wings. Whereupon Francis said, 'I believe it is pleasing to our Lord Jesus Christ that we should stay in this lonely mountain, seeing that our little sisters and brothers, the birds, show such joy at our arrival.' He began his fast on 15 August and was much troubled with temptation from the devil, as well as saddened by changes in the Order. The cross and passion of his Master were the special object of his devotions. He had spent the night before Holy Cross Day, 14 September, in prayer. 'In the morning he began to contemplate with exceedingly great devotion the passion of Christ, and his infinite love. Then Christ appeared to him on his cross, borne of angels, and said, "Do you know what I have done to you? I have given you the Stigmata, the signs of my passion, in order that you may be my standard bearer." ' Francis was filled with inexpressible joy, and then, when the vision disappeared, with physical agony. Looking to see the cause, he found in hands, feet and side the wounds of the Lord Jesus. However we may account for the Stigmata, it cannot be dismissed, for there is too much evidence to vouch for it. Francis had always set his face against singularity or any kind of excess amongst the brethren, and after receiving these marks he always covered his hands with the sleeves of his habit, and put on shoes and stockings.

Soon after his return to Portiuncula he fell sick with a complaint of the eyes. Before undergoing a very painful operation, he spent some time in a cell of reeds made by St Clare, in her convent garden. There he composed his famous Canticle of Brother Sun and the other Creatures of the Lord, a hymn of praise. He set it to music and taught the brothers to sing it. He underwent the operation which was calculated to cause excessive pain, but said he felt none. It was not successful, and he returned to Assisi to die in September 1225.

When told by the doctor that his death was near he said: 'Welcome, my Sister Death. If it pleases the Lord and I am so soon to die, call Brother Angelo and Brother Leo, that they may sing to me of Sister Death.' So they came and chanted the Song of Brother Sun, including some new verses on Sister Death. Brother Elias remonstrated, thinking such cheerfulness unseemly in the presence of death. Francis replied, 'Allow me, brother, to rejoice in the Lord, and in his praises, and in my own weakness, seeing that by the grace of the Holy Spirit I am so joined with the Lord that I may well be glad in him.'

He asked that he might be carried to the Portiuncula to die. On the way he had the litter stopped and himself lifted up, so that he might look on Assisi for the last time, and give it his blessing. He died on the night of 3 October 1226, praising God to the end. We are told that a multitude of larks 'came about the roof of the house where he lay and flying a little way off wheeled round the roof, and by their sweet singing appeared to be praising the Lord along with him'.

SHORT VERSION (*St Francis of Assisi*)

Perhaps the most famous of all Western Saints, Francis was born, lived much of his life and died in the hill city of Assisi in Umbria. His father was a rich cloth merchant who was infuriated beyond all reason when he discovered that his son had added to his other follies by selling cloth from the business in order to obtain money with which to repair the derelict church of St Damiano on the lower reaches of the city. Francis when praying in the church had heard the crucifix over the altar say 'Francis, go and repair my house, which you see is falling down.' Some years later Pope Innocent dreamt that St Peter's was collapsing, only being saved from destruction by a little man in a ragged grey tunic. The man was Francis, and the tunic that which he wore after he had renounced his home, and returned all his clothes to his father who had been trying to recoup in the bishop's court the money spent on San Damiano. Young men, many of them rich, joined Francis in his joyful pursuit of poverty and in 1210 this new order gained papal approval. Stories about Francis and his followers are legion, but in all of them run the themes of love of God, love of creation, and love of our Saviour, especially in his passion. Francis was determined to follow Christ as literally as possible and, in 1224 on Mount La Verna whilst in deep prayer, he saw a vision of the Crucified and received in his own hands, feet and sides, the wounds of the nails and the spear. Francis only lived a year after that experience, and as he was dying insisted that he should be stripped even of his rough tunic so that he might die like his Lord possessing nothing.

William Tyndale 6 OCTOBER
Translator of the Bible, 1536

It was while he was tutoring in Gloucestershire that William
Tyndale became aware of the great need for a translation of the
Bible into English. At university he had come under the
influence of Erasmus whose Greek edition of the New
Testament did much to prepare the ground for the
Reformation, and not only in England. Tyndale at first tried to
get support for his idea from the Church authorities in London,
but failure drove him to work abroad where it was safer. He
went to Germany in order to meet Martin Luther and, around
1526, a small first edition of his English translation of the New
Testament was printed in Cologne. Subsequent editions
followed and copies quickly found their way to England.
Church authorities did their best to prevent their circulation,
and Thomas More attacked the work on the grounds of
mistranslation, but such criticism can be largely discounted.
Tyndale remained safe in Germany, and by 1534 had published
a translation of the Old Testament as well. Attempts were
made to entice him back to England where he would
undoubtedly have been charged with heresy, but in 1535 while
in the Netherlands he was betrayed, tried and sentenced to
death. He was strangled and his body burnt at Vilworde in
October 1536 with a dying prayer on his lips, 'Lord, open the
King of England's eyes.'

St Paulinus

Missionary, 644

St Paulinus described by Bede as 'a man beloved of God', was consecrated bishop so that he could accompany the Princess Ethelburga, daughter of Ethelbert, the Christian King of Kent, when she married Edwin, the pagan King of Northumbria, 'so that by daily Mass and instruction he might preserve her and her companions from corruption by their constant association with the heathen'.

As soon as he entered the province, Paulinus began to work unceasingly for the conversion of the heathen; but although the king had renounced idol worship and allowed his infant daughter to be baptised in the Christian faith, being 'a wise and prudent man', he deliberated for a long time over which religion he should accept, and wished for further instruction from Paulinus. He also wanted to discuss the matter with his counsellors.

While the king hesitated, Paulinus one day approached him, and laying his hand on his head recalled to him a promise he had made in his youth: as a friendless exile he had been accosted by a stranger who promised him a kingdom and more power than any English king had yet known. The fulfilment of the promise depended on one condition, that Edwin should obey and follow the advice of one who would hereafter give him better and wiser guidance for life and salvation than any known hitherto. Edwin had given his word, and the stranger had laid his hand on the youth's head saying: 'When you receive this sign, remember this occasion . . . do not delay the fulfilment of your promise.' The stranger vanished, and Edwin knew him to have been a spirit.

At this reminder the king called his council and asked their opinion of the new faith. The high priest, Coifi, declared himself in favour of giving it a trial, since the old religion had not proved entirely reliable. Another of the chief men agreed, and went on to say: 'Your Majesty, when we compare the present life of man with that time of which we have no knowledge, it seems to me like the swift flight of a lone sparrow through the banqueting-hall where you sit in the winter months to dine with your thanes and counsellors. Inside there is a comforting fire to warm the room; outside, the wintry storms of snow and rain are raging. This sparrow flies swiftly in through one door of the hall, and out through another. While he is inside, he is safe from the winter storms; but after a few moments of comfort, he vanishes from sight into the darkness whence he came. Similarly, man appears on earth for a little while, but we know nothing of what went before this life, and what follows. Therefore if this new teaching can reveal any more certain knowledge, it seems only right that we should follow it.' The other elders and counsellors of the king, under God's guidance, gave the same advice.

Coifi led an assault on the heathen temple, desecrated it, and destroyed the altars. King Edwin was baptised at York with the chief men of his kingdom. Conversions followed rapidly. Paulinus baptised in the Swale, near Catterick, in the Glen, near Wooler in Northumberland, and at a pool near Hepple, in the same county, called Holywell ever since. He crossed the Humber and preached in Lindsey. At Lincoln he built a church dedicated to St Paul in which he consecrated St Honorius Archbishop of Canterbury. Bede tells us that Paulinus was a 'tall man, stooping a little, with black hair, thin face, and narrow, aquiline nose, venerable and awe-inspiring in appearance'.

After six years of rapid success his ministry in Northumbria came to an end. In 633 Edwin was killed in battle at Heathfield fighting against Penda of Mercia and Cadwalla of Wales. Paulinus left his deacon James in charge of York, and escorted Queen Ethelburga and her children to Kent by the sea route. He was already an elderly man, too old to contend with the chaos which reigned in Northumbria, and he accepted the bishopric of Rochester, occupying the see until his death on 10 October 644.

SHORT VERSION (*St Paulinus*)

King Edwin of Northumbria married the daughter of the Christian King Ethelbert of Kent and when Edwin's new Queen returned to the North with her husband, Paulinus was consecrated Bishop and sent with her. He quickly began preaching the gospel to Edwin's subjects but the King himself held back. One day however at council a bird flew into the chamber, flapped around for a bit and then disappeared through another window. One of the councillors likened the bird to a human being who appears on earth for a few years and at death goes into the unknown. He considered that if Christianity could shed light on what happens afterwards it was worth following. Thus the King and his council were baptised at York, and Paulinus began to expand his mission on as far as Lincoln where the remains of the Church that he built, known as St Paul's, have recently been excavated. Paulinus, after the death of Edwin, returned south where he became Bishop of Rochester and died there in 644.

St Edward the Confessor

King of England, 1066

Edward the Confessor was the son of Ethelred the Unready and was educated at the monastery of Ely, but spent most of his youth in Normandy until, at the age of forty, he was crowned in 1042.

After the quarrelling and oppressions of Harold and Hardicanute, he was welcomed by all his subjects. Devout and peace-loving, but far from being the weak, well-meaning character that he is sometimes represented, he was, in his own way, well able to cope with political pressures. William of Malmesbury has described him as 'a man by choice devoted to God, living the life of an angel in the administration of his kingdom'. He was also devoted to hunting and hawking, punctilious in the discharge of his religious duties, generous to the poor, and particularly hospitable to foreigners, doubtless because his early life was spent in Normandy.

He married, it is said in name only, Edith, the daughter of the Earl Godwin who had so ill-treated his brother Alfred as to cause his death. This may well have been a move of political expediency, since Godwin constituted the greatest danger to Edward. At one point in Edward's reign, Earl Godwin and his family were banished, and Queen Edith was shut away in a convent. In 1051 William of Normandy visited the English court, and may possibly have been offered the succession. Later the Godwins were received back into favour, and the king seems to have compromised with them in order to preserve the peace of the realm. Norman infuences were removed from the court, and the Norman Archbishop of Canterbury fled abroad. The harmony between the king and his council was so complete as to become the pattern for all succeeding reigns. Edward remitted the army-tax and gave the money to the poor.

In the years of exile, Edward had made a vow that he would take a pilgrimage to the tomb of St Peter in Rome, if God should please to mend the fortunes of his dynasty. At his accession he would have carried out his vow, but it was considered inexpedient for him to be absent from the kingdom for any length of time. The matter was referred to Pope Leo IX, who released the king from his vow on condition that the money which the expedition would have cost should be spent on the poor, and on the building and repair of a monastery in honour of St Peter.

Edward faithfully observed the conditions of his dispensation. The monastery chosen was an abbey on the west side of London. He rebuilt it and endowed it magnificently. It was commonly called West Minster, to distinguish it from the church of St Paul which lay to the east of the city. Westminster Abbey, rebuilt again in the thirteenth century, stands on the site of Edward's abbey church. The king was too ill to be present at the dedication ceremony. He died shortly afterwards and was buried in his new abbey where his shrine remains to this day.

SHORT VERSION (*St Edward the Confessor*)

Westminster Abbey, which he founded still houses the shrine of St Edward, son of Ethelred the Unready. Edward became King of England in 1042. He was not a particularly good monarch, though described by a chronicler as 'a man by choice devoted to God, living the life of an angel in the administration of his kingdom'. Before he came to his crown Edward had spent some years in exile during which he made a vow to visit the tomb of St Peter at Rome. However he was unable to leave England and, instead, Edward rebuilt Westminster Abbey in honour of the Saint. He was too ill to be present at the dedication of his new church but after his death in 1066 he was buried in it, and over a hundred years later his body was moved to its present shrine behind the High Altar.

St Teresa of Avila

Mystic, 1582

St Teresa was a Spaniard, born at Avila in Castile on 28 March 1515. Her parents were noble by birth and devout in character. She had three sisters and nine brothers, one of whom was her especial companion. When quite small they started on a pilgrimage to the Moors, in order that they might be martyred and reach heaven by a short road. They were amazed to read that the torments and glories of the next world were eternal, and delighted to repeat the words: 'for ever, for ever, for ever'. They made themselves hermitages in the garden, and when Teresa played with other little girls she loved to build monasteries. Afterwards, when her mother died, Teresa read romances, delighted in clothes, thought about her looks, and passed her time with frivolous acquaintances. Her father was displeased at this change and sent her to be educated in a convent under Augustinian rule, where she came under the influence of the sister who was in charge of the girls.

'Her good company soon began to banish all the habits evil company had led me into, and to restore my mind to the desire for eternal things, and also to some extent to remove the aversion I had felt to becoming a nun, an aversion which at one time was very great.'

She had to leave before long for reasons of health, but the impressions were permanent. In the year 1533, when she was eighteen, she decided to become a nun. Her father refused his consent, so she ran away from home, and entered the Convent of the Incarnation at Avila, belonging to the Carmelite order. For the first few years her health suffered, and she had to be taken away from the Convent more than once. The Convent belonged to a 'relaxed' order, which meant that the original stringency of its rule had been relaxed by papal dispensations, and she found the discipline too easy for the good of her soul. In spite of ill-health and relaxed discipline she began to train herself in prayer. Earlier, the *Letters of Saint Jerome* had enabled her to fix her desires on her vocation, and now the *Third Spiritual Alphabet*, by Father Francis de Osuna, came to her aid; but until she discovered the Jesuits, after being a nun for twenty years, she did not find a confessor who understood or helped her. The 'half-learned' and lenient did her most harm. She found concentration difficult, and could not pray without a book. At one time she dreaded the hour when it was time to pray, and would have preferred any penance to performing this obligation. Nevertheless she persisted, and received favours in prayer, and attained to heights of spiritual ecstasy that make her one of the greatest of mystics. Although her confessor thought her experiences a sign of divine favour, he advised her to resist them. She struggled against them for two months, but without success. Her visions are described by Teresa herself in her *Autobiography*, which she wrote at the command of her confessor.

In spite of great opposition, she founded a convent of strict, discalced (barefoot) nuns, dedicated to St Joseph, at Avila, on St Bartholomew's Day, 1562. Outstanding as a practical reformer, she has been described as a doctor of the spiritual life, and her writings, *The Way of Perfection*, *Foundations*, and *The Interior Castle*, are classics in the literature of mysticism.

It was said of her that 'In twenty years she had filled Spain with monasteries, in which more than a thousand religious praise God'. She herself combined cheerfulness with mortification to a wonderful degree, and her spirit was transfused into her nuns.

'Neither does labour weary them, neither confinement of the cloister irk them, nor sickness sadden them, nor does death affright or dismay them, but rather rejoice and cheer. The greatest marvel is the goodwill with which they do that which is hardest. Mortification is their delight, and resignation a sport, the harshness of penance a pastime, and they have turned the exercise of the heroic virtue to a pleasant diversion.'

In her novices she required intelligence even before piety, saying that an intelligent mind would see its faults and allow itself to be guided, whereas a less acute mind could never be brought to perceive its failings and was prone to complacency. 'May God preserve us from stupid nuns!'

She died at Alva while on a journey, 4 October 1582, and was buried there.

When she was eighteen Teresa ran away from home to the Carmelite Convent of the Incarnation at Avila. It belonged to the relaxed branch of the order and she remained there for over thirty years. In the face of much opposition she founded a convent of strict Carmelites in 1562, dedicated to St Joseph, and in twenty years had, so it was said, filled Spain with monasteries in which more than a thousand religious praised God. She herself combined cheerfulness with mortification to a wonderful degree, and her spirit was transfused into her nuns. In her novices Teresa preferred intelligence before piety, saying that an intelligent mind would see its faults and allow itself to be guided, whereas a less acute mind could never be brought to perceive its failings or if it was prone to complacency. 'May God preserve me from stupid nuns,' was her prayer. Teresa died on a journey at Alva in 1582.

St Ignatius

Bishop of Antioch, Martyr, 107

Ignatius was Bishop of Antioch for forty years, until the Emperor Trajan resumed the persecution of the Church as an act of gratitude to his gods for his victories. Ignatius was tried before him and condemned to be taken to Rome in fetters and there thrown to the wild beasts. The voyage followed the southern and western shores of Asia Minor, putting in at many ports and wherever the ship touched Christians flocked to receive the blessing of one who already appeared to them as a martyr. During the journey Ignatius wrote to the churches at Smyrna, Ephesus, Magnesia and Tralles, and his letters throw invaluable light on the early Christian Church, since they were written less than a century after the Ascension of our Lord. Ignatius warned the Churches against heresies. In his letter to the Church at Rome he implores the brethren to do nothing to avert his martyrdom. 'I fear your charity lest it prejudice me. For it is easy for you to do what you please; but it will be difficult for me to come to God unless you hold your hand. I shall never have another such opportunity of attaining unto my Lord . . . Therefore you cannot do me a greater favour than to suffer me to be poured out as a libation to God whilst the altar is ready; that, forming a choir in love, you may give thanks to the Father by Jesus Christ that God has vouchsafed to bring me, a Syrian bishop, from the east to the west to pass out of this world, that I may rise again unto him . . . But if I suffer I shall then become the freedman of Jesus Christ and in him I shall arise free." He died in the amphitheatre, devoured by two lions.

St Luke the Evangelist 18 OCTOBER

St Luke was a Gentile, almost certainly a Greek, from Syrian Antioch. He was a doctor. St Paul mentions him as 'my beloved physician', but we know nothing of his conversion. Author of a 'Gospel' and the 'Acts of the Apostles' Luke in the latter half of Acts gives the greatest prominence to Paul, whom he accompanied from the outset of his mission, and most of whose actions he witnessed. There are no reliable accounts of Luke after the death of Paul. A very ancient writer says that after serving his Master blamelessly, 'having neither child nor wife, he died in Bithynia at the age of seventy-four, filled with the Holy Spirit'. There is also a tradition that he was a painter as well as a physician, and he preached in Achaia.

St Simon and St Jude 28 OCTOBER
Apostles

St Simon Zelotes, was one of the Twelve. Nothing else is known of him. The word Zelotes means 'the Zealous', but it is not by any means certain that he belonged to the sect of the Zealots. The eastern Church holds that he died naturally at Edessa. The western tradition is that he preached in Egypt, worked with St Jude when he came from Mesopotamia, and that they went to Persia and were martyred there. Jude may be the brother of James the Less. After the Last Supper it was Jude who asked our Lord why he chose to manifest himself only to his followers. He received the reply that to any who loved him 'we will come to him and will make our home with him'. The epistle which bears the name of Jude is addressed generally to the Church and warns against undesirable elements which had crept in.

James Hannington

Bishop of East Equatorial Africa, Missionary, Martyr, 1885

On 17 May 1882 James Hannington, having been ordained for only eight years found himself on a ship sailing for East Africa and bound for the CMS Mission in Zanzibar. Ill health brought him back after a year, but in 1884 he was consecrated in Lambeth Parish Church to be the Bishop in East Equatorial Africa. Once again he sailed for that continent. He travelled widely through his huge diocese, always being in the forefront of any new development. It was while he was in Uganda that he was taken prisoner by Mwanga, the ruler of those parts, and killed on 28 April 1885, along with the majority of his companions.

Saints and Martyrs of the Reformation Era   31 OCTOBER

This commemoration might include:

St John Fisher, *Bishop, Martyr, 1535*

John Fisher was Bishop of Rochester when Henry VIII engineered the breach with Rome. Alongside Thomas More, with whom he was sent to The Tower in 1534, he refused to take the oath which acknowledged the King as Supreme Head of the Church in England, and on 22 June 1535 he was beheaded on Tower Hill.

John Rogers, *Priest, Martyr, 1555*

He had been Vicar of St Sepulchre's in London and was thrown into the Tower of London when Mary became Queen. On the day of his burning he told the sheriff who asked him to change his mind, 'That which I have preached, I will seal with my blood'. 'You are a heretic then', said the sheriff, 'and I will never pray for you.' 'But I will pray for you,' replied Rogers. He died on 4 February 1555.

St Margaret Clitheroe, *Wife, Martyr, 1586*

During the reign of Elizabeth I the laws against recusants were enforced more strictly particularly after the Pope had declared it to be a good Christian act to murder the Queen. Many English Catholics suffered as a result, among them Margaret Clitheroe, wife of a Protestant butcher in York. In March 1580 their home was searched and the secret chapel where several Latin Masses had been regularly celebrated was discovered. Margaret was brought for trial but she refused to reply to the charge and therefore was executed by being pressed to death. Her feast day is 21 October.

Hugh Latimer, and Nicholas Ridley, *Bishops, Martyrs, 1555*

These two are perhaps the most famous of the Marian martyrs, by reason of Latimer's encouragement to his fellow sufferer at the stake in Oxford. 'Be of good comfort Master Ridley, and play the man. We shall this day light such a candle, by God's grace, in England, as I trust shall never be put out.'

146

Richard Hooker
3 NOVEMBER

Teacher of the Faith, 1600

Richard Hooker is the first great systematic Anglican theologian. In 1585 he was appointed Master of the Temple in London where he remained until 1591 when he retired to Boscombe and Bishopsborne in order to complete his famous book *Ecclesiastical Polity*. It is for this that he is chiefly remembered. In it he provides a fundamental basis for an Anglican approach to the Christian Way and especially in the relationships between Church and State.... 'Since there can be no goodness desired which proceedeth not from God Himself, as from the supreme cause of all things; and every effect doth after a sort contain, at leastwise resemble, the cause from which it proceedeth: all things in the world are said in some sort to seek the highest, and to covet more or less the participation of God Himself.' Book V provides one of the best commentaries on the Prayer Book, and in Book VI, which he never completed, Hooker upheld an episcopally ordered Church.

Saints and Martyrs of England
8 NOVEMBER

There are so many who do not find a place in the Calendar: the well-known like St Richard of Chichester, the not so well known like St Gilbert of Sempringham, Founder of the first English pre-Reformation Community, St Alphege and William Laud, Martyr Archbishops of Canterbury, St Frideswide, Abbess, now protectress of Fleet Street, St Willibrord, the Saxon missionary to Friesland (now Holland), not to mention those great men and women who went out from this country in the nineteenth century. In later times too, Richard Benson, Founder of Cowley Fathers, and William Temple, another Archbishop of Canterbury. The list is endless and in the end must be very personal. There is space enough ...

St Martin
Bishop of Tours, 397

11 NOVEMBER

St Martin was born at Sabaria, in Pannonia. His family were pagans, and his father was a soldier who wished his son to follow the same career, and entered him in the army at the age of fifteen.

Martin disliked the prospect of soldiering. All his inclinations were towards the life of the cloister. He wished to become a Christian, and during his five years as a serving officer he contrived to lead an almost monkish life, a considerable achievement at any period of history. He shared his tent and his meals with his servant, and helped him in his duties.

One day, in the bitter cold of a severe winter, he saw a pauper at the city gate of Amiens, shivering with cold and begging alms without success. Martin had no money to give, but he took off his cloak, cut it in half with his sword, and gave half to the beggar. That night he dreamed of Christ, surrounded by angels, wearing the half-cloak he had given to the beggar; 'See', he said, 'this is the cloak which Martin has given me.'

Martin was baptized at Amiens. After serving for five years against the invading Germans, he asked to be released from further military service. He refused his war bounty from Juliun Caesar, saying, 'Hitherto I have served you as a soldier. Let me now serve Christ.' He was accused of cowardice, and retorted by offering to stand unarmed in the battle-line and advance on the enemy alone in the name of Christ. He was imprisoned, but was released at the end of the German war.

He became a disciple of St Hilary of Poitiers. Instructed in a dream to visit his parents he returned to Pannonia where he converted his mother and several others, but not his father. He opposed the Arians in Illyricum with such vigour that he was publicly scourged and driven from the country. Hearing that the Church of Gaul was in Arian control and Hilary banished, he remained at Milan for some time. Driven from Milan by the Arian bishop, he took refuge on an island in the Gulf of Genoa, where he remained until Hilary was recalled to his see.

Hilary gave Martin a piece of land, to which he attracted a number of disciples. This community grew into a great

148

monastery, the first to be founded in Gaul, and it was still in existence over fourteen centuries later. In 371 the people of Tours clamoured for Martin as their bishop. He was so reluctant that they captured him by a strategem, luring him to visit a sick woman, seizing him and carrying him before the bishops. These were quite as averse to the whole affair as its victim, considering Martin an unsuitable candidate for the see on the score of his neglected and disreputable appearance. Their objections were over-ruled by the clergy and populace, and he was consecrated.

Martin now ruled a mainly pagan diocese, but his instruction and the example of his life prevailed. He destroyed temples and idols, and worked a great number of miracles. In one instance the priests agreed to fell their idol, a large fir tree, if Martin would stand directly in the path of its fall. They would then know beyond all doubt whether his God or theirs were the stronger. The fir was cut, it leaned, toppled, and was about to fall on the bishop, when he made the sign of the cross, and it swerved and fell to one side. He travelled his diocese annually, on foot, by boat and by donkey, but his influence extended far beyond his own terrain.

In order to avoid the crowds who sought him out, Martin retired to a cell on a steep cliff. He was joined by eighty disciples, who lived there in great austerity. This was the beginning of the abbey of Marmoutier.

Martin was frequently honoured with visions. On one occasion he was tempted by Satan in the guise of Christ in glory. Bur Martin, looking in vain for the marks of the Passion, was not to be deceived.

When Avitianus, a notoriously cruel officer of the Imperial Guard, arrived with a batch of prisoners who were to be tortured and executed the next day, Martin interceded for them and secured their release. His compassion led to a curious situation in the year 384. The heretic Priscillian and six companions had been condemned by the Emperor Maximus. The bishops who had condemned them in the ecclesiastical court insisted on their execution. Martin contended that the secular power had no authority to condemn, and that excommunication by the bishops was an adequate sentence. In this he was upheld by St Ambrose, Bishop of Milan. He refused to leave

Treves until the emperor promised to reprieve them. No sooner was his back turned, than the bishops persuaded the emperor to break his promise; Priscillian and his followers were executed. This was the first occasion of heresy being punished by death.

Martin was justifiably furious, and he publicly excommunicated the bishops responsible. But afterwards he took them back into communion in exchange for a pardon from Maximus for certain men condemned to death, and for the emperor's promise to end the persecution of the remaining Priscillianists. He never felt easy in his mind about this concession, and thereafter avoided assemblies of bishops at which he might encounter some of those concerned in the affair. When eighty years old, and longing for his rest, he was persuaded by his disciples to pray for longer life; 'Lord, if I am still necessary to your people, I do not refuse the toil.' The prayer was not granted, and he died on 9 November 401 at Candes.

SHORT VERSION (*St Martin*)

Martin during his service career in the Roman army was on his way back to his barracks. It was a bitter winter's day and at the gate of Amiens, he met a beggar shivering with the cold. Martin had no money so he took off his cloak, cut it in half with his sword and gave half to the beggar. That night in his dreams, Martin saw Jesus Christ surrounded by angels, wearing the half-cloak, and he heard Christ say 'See, this is the cloak which Martin has given me.' Martin had long been considering baptism and this finally convinced him. In 371 the Christians of Tours, much against his will, chose him as their new bishop, and he remained as such for thirty years, proving himself a champion of the under-dog and an unflagging and courageous missionary. He died in 401.

Charles Simeon

Pastor, Preacher, 1836

Few priests remain in a single place all their working lives, but Charles Simeon did. He was ordained in 1782 and appointed to Holy Trinity, Cambridge in 1783, where he was minister for fifty-five years. He himself wrote of a particular Lent as a student at King's College, 'On 29 January 1879 I came to college. On 2 February I understood that at division of term I must attend the Lord's Supper. The Provost absolutely required it. Conscience told me that, if I must go, I must repent and turn to God, unless I chose to enter and drink my own damnation. From that day I never ceased to mourn and pray, till I obtained progressive manifestation of God's mercy in Christ in Passion Week, and perfect peace on Easter Day, 4 April.' Throughout his long ministry Charles wanted to share that experience of peace with all who came to him. It was not always easy; his churchwardens, to begin with, were not encouraging, and many in the parish and university were hostile to his Evangelical zeal. He exercised an enormous influence on many undergraduates, and was also one of the founders of CMS. In his lifetime and afterwards, his loyalty to the Church of England and her worship was often questioned but without any justification. He died in 1836.

St Margaret of Scotland

16 NOVEMBER

Queen, Wife and Mother, 1093

She was escaping from England and the Norman conquerors, when her boat was driven on to the Northumbrian coast and into the realm of King Malcolm. She was a Saxon Princess and so provided cogent reason why she would make a good match for the king. He, also, fell in love with her and theirs remained a happy marriage. Margaret had enormous influence over her husband. The Church in Scotland still clung to the old Celtic ways; Margaret looked to the Church on the Continent and Rome. She encouraged a change of attitude especially on the part of the clergy, and at Dumferline she introduced Benedictine monks into Scotland. She died in Edinburgh Castle on 16 November 1093, after having heard of the death in battle of both her husband and her eldest son.

St Hilda

Abbess of Whitby, 680

St Hilda was the daughter of Hereric, nephew of St Edwin, King of Northumbria. When she was thirteen she was baptized by St Paulinus, with her uncle. Bede relates that when Hilda was in her infancy her mother had a dream in which she searched for her banished husband. 'When all her efforts had failed, she discovered a most valuable jewel under her garments, and as she looked closely it emitted such a brilliant light that all Britain was lit by its splendour. This dream was fulfilled in her daughter . . .'

After living for thirty-three years 'most nobly in the secular habit', she renounced the world and retired to East Anglia, which was ruled by her cousin, King Anna. She intended to travel to Gaul, where her sister Hereswitha was a nun in the monastery of Chilles, near Paris, but after a year Bishop Aidan recalled her to Northumbria and granted her one hide of land on the north bank of the River Wear. She settled there in a small nunnery, until she was made abbess of the double monastery of Hartlepool.

After reorganising the monastery, she passed on to Tadcaster (probably) and being appointed abbess, 'quickly set herself to establish a regular observance as she had been instructed by learned men: for Bishop Aidan and other devout men, who knew her and admired her innate wisdom and love of God, often used to visit and advise her'. Later, Hilda was appointed to found, or possibly reorganise, the monastery of Whitby. This monastery became noted as a school of learning and religion. The great Synod of Whitby was held there in 664 to decide the date of Easter, and other contested matters. St Hilda favoured the Celtic usages, but she obediently accepted the contrary decision of the synod.

Caedmon, the poet, was an out door servant of the monastery. His gift was bestowed on him as he lay in the stable among the animals in his charge. When he was brought before Hilda, 'the abbess was delighted that God had given such grace to the man, and advised him to abandon the secular life and adopt the monastic state'. She also assisted his education.

For the last six years of her rule she was racked continually by a burning fever, which she bore with patience and courage. In the seventh year she died.

SHORT VERSION (*St Hilda*)
Like so many of the early Saints of Britain, Hilda was of royal birth. She only became a nun when she was thirty-three. She lived in several abbeys in the North East finally settling at Whitby, where she either founded or reorganised an abbey of both men and women, and which she ruled until she died. Caedmon, the first remembered poet in English was encouraged by her. She died in 680 sixteen years after the Synod of Whitby where, sadly for Hilda and her community, the Church in England decided on the Roman method for fixing Easter rather than the old Celtic use.

St Hugh

Bishop of Lincoln, 1200

St Hugh was a member of a noble Burgundian family. His father, William, Lord of Avalon, was a soldier who ended his days as a religious at the convent of Villard-Benoit, where his son was educated. Hugh was always intended for monastic life. He knew none of the ordinary pleasure of childhood, and in the monastery school he was not allowed to play with other boys. 'Let them alone', his father used to say, 'study is better suited to you.' At the age of nineteen he was ordained deacon, and quickly established a reputation as a preacher.

He accompanied his prior on a visit to the Grande Chartreuse. There the peace and silence of the place roused in him a great longing for the contemplative life, and an intention to take the habit of that most austere Order. He met with some opposition from his superior at Villard-Benoit, but he returned to the Chartreuse and was admitted. He spent ten years in his cell, until he was appointed procurator of the monastery, an office which he held for seven years.

As part of his penance for the murder of St Thomas Becket, Henry II had founded the first Carthusian monastery in England, at Witham, in Somerset. Under the two first priors, difficulties had arisen which made it impossible to establish the monastery. A French noble had recommended the monk Hugh for the office, and the Bishop of Bath was sent to France to interest the chapter of the Grande Chartreuse to part with him. Protesting that he was unequal to the responsibility, Hugh was ordered to accompany the bishop to England.

On his arrival Hugh found that the building of the monastery had not begun. Worse, no compensation had been paid to those who would have to lose their lands and property to make room for it. Hugh refused to take office until all these people had been compensated. Completion of the actual building was held up once more because Henry was in debt to the builders. Hugh brought diplomacy to bear on this awkward situation, and the first English Charterhouse was established.

Henry loved him for his plain speaking. 'I do not despair of you', Hugh said to him at their first interview; 'I know how much your many occupations interfere with the health of your soul.' Henry, delighted, swore that while he lived he should not leave his kingdom, and took so much pleasure in his conversation, and paid such heed to his counsels that a rumour arose that Hugh was his son. Hugh's biographer and chaplain wrote that 'of all men only Hugh could bend that rhinoceros to his will.' When Henry was in danger of shipwreck, he cried out, 'If only my Carthusian Hugh were awake and at prayer, God would not forget me.'

This affection never diminished, though Hugh dared to oppose the king, particularly in the matter of keeping sees vacant in order to draw their revenues. One of the worst examples was Lincoln which, except for a few months, had been without a bishop for eighteen years. Hugh was elected, and the prior of the Grande Chartreuse overrode his objections and obliged him to submit to consecration as bishop. After such a long period of neglect, there was great need of reform. Hugh employed priests of great piety and learning, and made the fullest use of his authority in disciplining his clergy. He took a stern view of the ill-treatment of the poor by the royal foresters, and when a subject of the church of Lincoln suffered at their hands he excommunicated their chief. He also refused a prebend for a courtier.

Henry was furious, and summoned him to his presence. He came, and Henry turned away his face and would not speak, but by way of ignoring his presence took out a torn glove and began to sew it. At last Hugh said, 'How like you are to your relations at Falaise.' The king might have resented this allusion to the humble birth of William the Conqueror's mother, the glove-maker's daughter, but he only laughed, and the quarrel was made up.

Jew-baiting broke out in England at the time of the Third Crusade. In defence of the persecuted, Hugh faced armed mobs in Lincoln, Stamford and Northampton and compelled their submission.

Hugh was on good terms with Richard I but his relations with King John were less happy. When John expressed his good intentions, Hugh said bluntly, 'You know I hate lies', and warned him against promising what he did not intend to perform. John showed him an amulet, which he said was sacred and would preserve his dominions. 'Do not', replied Hugh, 'put your trust in lifeless stone, but only in the living and heavenly stone, our Lord Jesus Christ.' The following Easter he preached at some length on the duties of kings. John, liking neither the matter nor the length of the sermon, sent three times to tell him to bring it to a close. Hugh disregarded these broad hints and went on to the end. The king slipped out without communicating, as he did at his coronation on the following Ascension Day.

At that time the diocese of Lincoln stretched as far south as Oxford and Slough. Under Hugh, it became a pattern of wise episcopal administration. His courageous refusal of a levy to subsidise a war of Richard I was the first clear case of a refusal of a money grant to the Crown. It created a most valuable precedent. Just before taking this perilous stand, the bishop had been confirmed in his resolution by a vision granted to one of his young clerics.

Devout, tirelessly industrious, self-denying and disinterested, Hugh had all the characteristics demanded of a saint. He also had wit, a temper which he himself described as 'more biting than pepper', and a great and unaffected love for the poor and helpless, particularly for small children. He worked many miracles, but attached no importance to them. He visited leper-houses and washed the sores of their inmates. His generosity was unbounded.

Hugh's love for animals is well known. At Chartreuse birds and squirrels fed from his hands. At Witham he had a tame goose. At Stow, one of the manors of Lincoln, he had a wild swan which would feed from his hand, follow him about, and keep guard over his bed, so that it was impossible for anyone to approach him without being attacked by it.

His greatest refreshment was to return to Witham when he could escape from his duties. There he would live as an ordinary monk, strictly observing the rule of the community.

In 1200 the king sent him to France on matters of state. He was received everywhere with joy and veneration, but he contracted an illness and returned to England to die, while attending a council in London. He lingered for two months, in patient endurance of pain, at his house in the Old Temple, Holborn (Lincoln's Inn) and died there on the evening of 16 November 1200.

When he was fifty-one Hugh was elected Bishop of Lincoln in 1186. Up to that date and from boyhood he had lived in various monasteries, and was Prior of the Charterhouse at Witham in Somerset at the time of his election. The diocese had been neglected for years. Hugh proved to be a bishop of reforming zeal, outspoken even to kings when they needed correction. He defended the Jews when anti-semitism broke out both in Lincoln and other parts of his enormous diocese, and was a man of unbounded generosity, particularly to the poor. Hugh died in London returning from a diplomatic mission he had undertaken for the King in France in the year 1200.

St Edmund of East Anglia

King, Martyr, 870

St Edmund, said to have been a Saxon prince, was appointed by Offa, King of East Anglia, as his successor. He set sail from Kent and was shipwrecked off the coast of Norfolk, at a place still known as St Edmund's Point. He was fourteen when the nobles and clerics acknowledged him king at Attleburgh. During the year of his probation, he is said to have learned the psalter by heart, in order to join in the worship of the Church, and to emulate King David. At that time the Danes were not only raiding England frequently, but they were beginning to spend their winters there. In the year 866, the greatest invasion of all penetrated East Anglia but they only took up winter quarters along the coast. The East Angles, however, collaborated, supplying them with horses; so they took York and marched south as far as Nottingham. The next year they crossed Mercia and settled at Thetford, where the winter following Edmund fought them, and lost. He was offered peace on condition that he halved his treasure with the Danes and became a vassal prince. Edmund would have complied with the first condition, but not the second. He refused to become a vassal unless his overlord would become a Christian. He believed that he had been called to this office by God, in order to advance Christ's kingdom. As the vassal of a heathen this would be impossible. The Danish prince Hingmar ordered Edmund to be scourged and tied to a tree as a living target for his archers. Then he was dragged from the tree and beheaded. His body was thrown aside in the forest, but it was discovered afterwards under the miraculous guidance of a grey wolf. It was taken up and buried at Hoxne, and in the year 903 transferred to Bury St Edmunds.

St Andrew the Apostle

St Andrew, the first Apostle to be called by our Lord, was the son of Jona, a fisherman. His brother was Simon Peter and they were natives of Bethsaida, in Galilee. Andrew, at least, was a disciple of St John the Baptist. When John, after baptising Jesus, said, 'Behold the Lamb of God,' Andrew and one other disciple followed our Lord, and the same day knew that he was the Messiah. Andrew's first act was to call his brother, Simon, who was admitted to discipleship, and given the name of Peter. From that time the two brothers were intermittently with Jesus. On one occasion they baptised in the river Jordan with his authority. Later, Jesus called them from their fishing, saying that he would make them fishers of men. At the feeding of the five thousand it was Andrew who told Jesus about the boy with the barley loaves and the fishes. When some Greeks desired to see Jesus, they went to Philip; Philip told Andrew and the two went to Jesus. According to Eusebius, Andrew preached in Scythia. Other writers mention him as evangelising in Epirus and in Achaia. These traditions are perfectly probable. Less so, is the claim that he reached Byzantium. He is said to have been crucified at Patras, in Achaia, being first scourged and then bound to a diagonal cross in order that his sufferings might be prolonged. The story relates that Andrew preached from the cross to twenty thousand men, and lingered for two days before he died. His hearers felt, 'this bold and debonair man ought not to suffer thus', and many were converted.

Nicholas Ferrar

Deacon, Founder of the Little Gidding Community, 1637

Nicholas Ferrar was a cockney, having been born not far from the present offices of the Bible Society in Queen Victoria Street.

His father was a prosperous merchant, whose business was carried on in Europe, India, and America, which was called at that time, The New World. He was a member of the Virginia Company which controlled the Government as well as the trade of the new colony, and when his time came to retire, his place was taken by Nicholas. In 1624, thirteen years after its foundation by Royal Charter, the Company was dissolved, although Nicholas, who had served it as Deputy Treasurer, during the last years of its existence, tried very hard to prevent the dissolution. One wealthy member asked Nicholas to marry his daughter. With the lady, her father was prepared to give £10,000 as her dowry. 'I shall never marry,' was his reply. 'As soon as the affairs of the Virginia Company are settled, I intend to give my life wholly to serving God.'

It was about this time, too, that he became a Member of Parliament. His work there, together with his duties during the winding up of the Virginia Company, brought him to the notice of King James and his Council. He was offered two important Government posts, but he refused. He and his family were determined to live away from London to devote their days to continual worship.

They needed a house large enough for the whole family, which included Nicholas' mother, sister and her husband. He began to make enquiries and eventually found the house and church at Little Gidding. It suited them exactly, being some distance from the main part of the village, Great Gidding. The church had been allowed to fall into disrepair—when the family arrived it was used as a haycroft and the sacristy as a pigsty. The house itself had never been looked after properly by the previous owner, and was in a very bad condition.

Before they finally left London, Nicholas was ordained Deacon in Westminster Abbey. The family remained in London for just one more week and then went back to begin the special life together which was to continue uninterrupted, and with few changes, until nine years after the death of Nicholas. It would be a mistake to think of Little Gidding as a kind of monastery or convent, although during and even before the Civil War the Puritans often called it that.

The day's work revolved around the church, to which they all went four times a day. In between these services, they held in a large room in the house a short service every hour. Not everyone went to these, but the household was divided into bands and each band took it in turns to say the hourly service. This meant, of course, that every waking hour of the day had its own worship. At night time some of the family kept a watch, and the whole of the Psalter was recited. Nicholas, during the latter part of his life rarely spent more than three hours in bed each night.

Apart from ordinary household duties, the children used to go to school and learn all the subjects that were usually taught in those days. Three times a week the family provided food for the poor folk of the district, and Nicholas ran a surgery for them, as he had learnt a great deal about medicine when he was at university.

During the hourly services they used to read through the four Gospels. In order that they might read through our Lord's life as one continuous story, but so that they would not miss out anything written about him, they made a large Harmony of the Four Gospels. It was rather like a big scrap-book, and in it they pasted, in the right order, all the stories cut out from many copies of the New Testament. In between the printed passages they stuck appropriate prints to illustrate the stories. Nicholas had once collected these prints during his travels through Holland, Spain, Italy and Austria. When the book was finished it was beautifully bound in leather and became a family treasure. A second one was made for King Charles I, and this copy is now in the British Library.

The little community survived the death of Nicholas in 1637, but it was finally dispersed by Oliver Cromwell's soldiers in 1645.

SHORT VERSION (*Nicholas Ferrar*)
Historians looking for early revivals of the Religious Life in

England after the Reformation often refer to the family community of Little Gidding, founded there by Nicholas Ferrar in 1625. His family had been involved in the Virginia Company, but they determined to leave London and settle in the country to follow a life of prayer. The tiny church at Little Gidding in Huntingdonshire became their daily chapel, and in the farmhouse they had an oratory where one member of the household was always keeping watch. The watch was continued throughout the night when the whole of the Psalter was recited. The little community was visited by Charles I, who liked what he saw, and naturally was considered a papist stronghold by the Puritans; but it survived the death of Nicholas in 1637 only to be dispersed by Cromwell's troops in 1645.

Saints and Martyrs of Asia

St Francis Xavier, *Missionary, 1552*

St Francis Xavier was born near Pamplona, at the Castle of Xavier, in 1506. His father was Juan de Jasso, a nobleman of Navarre. Francis took his name from his mother, who had brought the property of Xavier into the family. He was the youngest of several children.

At the age of eighteen Francis went to the University of Paris, where he took the degree of Master of Arts and became a lecturer in logic and metaphysics. One of the students who attended his lectures was a fellow Basque, Ignatius Loyola, who tried to win his friendship. At first Francis resisted, then he capitulated and became one of the band of seven, the original Jesuits, who took their vows at Montmartre. With them he was ordained priest seven years later at Venice, and was sent out in 1540 on the first missionary expedition to the East Indies with Father Simon Roderiguez.

Simon Roderiguez had gone ahead, and was already in Lisbon, working in a hospital. Francis joined him there and shared his labours. The King of Portugal, John III, was so much impressed by the two priests that he detained them, Roderiguez permanently, and Francis for eight months. When Francis was finally allowed to set sail on 7 April 1541, he carried the authority of papal nuncio. His two companions were Father Camerino and Father Mansilhas.

The voyage took thirteen months. They were anything but idle months for Francis. The ship carried a cross section of humanity: slaves, merchants, soldiers, and the ship's crew. He mixed and talked with them freely, catechised, preached, heard confessions and nursed the sick. There was an outbreak of scurvy on board and Francis turned his cabin into an infirmary. He had refused to have a servant, preferring to wash and cook and mend for himself, rather than depend on another. A Portuguese passenger was scandalized at the manner in which he mixed on genial and familiar terms with all sorts and conditions of men. He set his servant to watch the Padre Santo when they landed. The man followed the priest to a wood, where he saw him lifted from the ground in an ecstasy of prayer.

Francis landed at Goa, in India, on 6 May 1542. The Portuguese had been established there for thirty-two years, and in that time, climate, opportunity, and lack of communication with their own country, had considerably demoralised the settlers. Their treatment of slaves was appalling, the sacraments were neglected, there were no priests outside the city, and the behaviour of the Europeans was not likely to recommend their faith to the heathen.

Francis commenced his mission amongst the settlers. He visited the prisons and hospitals (almost indistinguishable in their squalor), offered Mass among the lepers, and walked the streets ringing a bell to call the children for religious instruction. His method with natives, the young and the uninstructed, was to teach them (in the vernacular) the truths of Christianity in verse composed by himself and set to popular tunes. These were no sooner heard than memorised, and sung everywhere. In dealing with the peculiar difficulties and failings of exiles living in small communities in an alien continent, Francis showed humanity and tact, and a most practical approach to their problems.

In the first six years in India he visited the Portuguese settlements along the coast from Goa to Cape Comorin, and from Comorin to Negapatam and Meliapur, where he found relics of St Thomas, who was said to have been martyred there. He sailed East as far as the Celebes and the Molucca Islands, indefatigable in caring for the Portuguese, as well as in converting the natives. Each centre that he established would be regularly visited by himself or another Jesuit father. Sometimes he could hardly lift his hands, from the fatigue of baptising so many.

Francis has been described by one of his companions: 'He is a father; no one can see him without great consolation, the very sight of him seems to move to devotion; he is a man of middle height, he always holds his face up, his eyes are full of tears, but his look is bright and joyous, his words few. His very look kindles in men an inexpressible desire to serve God.'

All those who came in contact with him were affected by his singular charm, and the unaffected courtesy which had its roots in his concern for others and his love for humanity. He wrote that the sufferings of the native peoples had become a permanent bruise on his soul. He wrote to the King of Portugal in terms not usually employed to kings: '... it is possible that when our Lord God calls your Highness to his Judgement that your Highness may hear angry words from him: "Why did you not punish those who were your subjects and owned your authority, and were enemies to me in India?" ' Francis was alluding to the danger of native converts falling from their new faith in revulsion from the treatment which they received under Portuguese domination.

Francis himself lived on rice and water, slept only for four hours, lying on the ground with a stone for his head. He spent the rest of his nights in prayer or in visiting the sick. He performed many miracles of healing, and was honoured with such religious ecstasy that he was sometimes forced to exclaim: 'Lord, give me not so much joy in this life; or if, in your mercy, you must heap it upon me, take me all together to yourself.' On his return from Japan he was several times observed walking in the garden at night, and heard to cry out, 'No more, O Lord, no more!'—feeling the intensity of divine consolation almost more than he could bear.

Like many other saints, Francis was a man of affairs, as well as a mystic. More than a hundred of his letters survive, dealing among other things, with practical matters. They contain excellent advice on preaching, on administering rebukes to highly-placed officials (he had a great talent for this), on dealing with penitents who came 'to reveal their indigence rather than their sins', who were to be kept at a distance as 'drones who would rob you of your store', on the management of finance, with very precise and detailed instructions on the recovery of borrowed money. He even dealt with housekeeping and the garden. No details were too small for his attention. He took great pains to learn the dialects of those he wished to convert. He is popularly believed to have had an almost miraculous gift for languages, but there is no foundation for this, and some authorities hold the contrary view.

In 1515 St Francis visited the Malay Peninsula and spent four months in the city of Malacca. He visited islands where there were Portuguese settlements, and was exposed to much hardship and many dangers. In Malaya it first occurred to him to go to Japan. Although he spent the next year in India, visiting the widely scattered mission outposts which he had established, he was busy preparing to take up the challenge which Japan presented. In 1549 he set out for Japan, accompanied by five helpers: a Jesuit priest and a lay-preacher, and three Japanese converts.

The voyage was perilous as, apart from the danger of the sea, there was always a chance that if the winds were unfavourable, he and his companions would be thrown overboard as bringers of ill-luck. This nearly happened more than once, and Francis, writing to his brethren at Goa, gave advice on how to combat 'this plague of timidity which makes many men lead a sad and anxious life'. His remedy was trust in God.

He landed at Kagoshima, on 15 August 1549, and ultimately penetrated as far as Miyako. The missionaries met with mixed treatment; in Kagoshima, a year of teaching resulted in a hundred converts, after which further preaching was forbidden by the authorities. At Ichiku, the small, isolated community of the fortress were converted and, visited twelve years later by a Jesuit, were found to be still practising the faith with ardour. At Hirado they were welcomed by the ruler; in Honshu they were reviled. In Miyako, Francis approached the ruler more as the envoy of a temporal power than as a missionary. He gave him presents and letters from the Goanese authorities, and in return was permitted to preach, and given the use of an empty Buddhist Monastery. Francis, the first to teach the Gospel in Japan, made perhaps two thousand converts. They, and their succeeding generations, have shown a constancy under persecution which has never been surpassed.

On his return to India in 1552, Francis found that good progress had been made, but for four months he was occupied in solving the difficulties and irregularities which had inevitably occurred during his absence. After setting things in order he sailed for China, accompanied by a Jesuit father, four lay brothers, and a young Chinese who was to act as interpreter.

It had been arranged that Francis, as papal nuncio, should accompany Pereira, the Portuguese ambassador, to wait upon the Chinese embassy. But the maritime authority at Malacca refused Pereira permission to sail, and the embassy had to be abandoned. Pereira unselfishly agreed to allow Francis to sail for China in his ship. In the end Francis decided to attempt a secret landing in Canton, and sent away all his helpers except Anthony, the Chinese. On the desolate island of Sancian they waited for a Chinese trader who had agreed to put them ashore on the mainland. The trader never came, and at the end of November Francis was stricken with fever. He died on 2 December 1552. Anthony has described his master's last moments, in a letter: 'I could see that he was dying, and put a lighted candle in his hand. Then, with the name of Jesus on his lips, he rendered his soul to his Creator and Lord, in peace.'

SHORT VERSION (*St Francis Xavier*)
Francis Xavier, one of the first followers of St Ignatius Loyola, founder of the Society of Jesus, is sometimes called 'the Apostle to the Indies'. He came from Navarre, then a kingdom, now part of France, and when he was at university in Paris came under the influence of St Ignatius. In 1541 he set out for India and landed at Goa thirteen months later. He was never to return to Europe but during the next ten years spent himself in preaching the gospel, not only throughout India, but also in Ceylon, Malaya, China and Japan. He died on an island off the Chinese mainland in 1552. One of his companions wrote of him as a 'true father, no one can see him without being comforted, the very sight of him seems to move to devotion . . . his look kindles in men an inexpressible desire to serve God'.

Martyrs of Japan, *16th and 17th Centuries*

St Francis Xavier first preached Christ in Japan in 1549, and by 1587, it is said, there were over 20,000 Christians in Japan. However in 1597 three Jesuits and six Franciscans were crucified on a hill outside Nagasaki. Twenty four others followed them to death and in the following century during further persecution over 200 martyrs suffered. The torments devised for the martyrs were most horrible and many took a long time to die. Yet all but a very few remained faithful to the end.

Twentieth Century Saints of Asia also include the Boxer Martyrs in China, St Nicholas of Japan; Martyrs of Burma; Bishop Samuel Azariah of South India.

168

St Nicholas

6 DECEMBER

Bishop of Myra, c.326

St Nicholas is believed to have been born at Patara in Asia Minor. He became Bishop of Myra in the fourth century, and was famous for his piety and his many miracles. The least unreliable account of his life was written by St Methodius, Patriarch of Constantinople, in the ninth century.

The legends of Nicholas are many. It came to his notice that an impoverished citizen of Patara was about to turn his three daughters into the streets (being unable to give them a marriage dowry). Nicholas saved them from prostitution. On three nights he threw a bag of gold through an open window of the citizen's house, enabling him to secure a husband for each girl.

The governor of the Province of Lycia had accepted a bribe to condemn three innocent men to death. Nicholas attended the execution at the appointed hour, stopped it, and set the prisoners free. Then he turned upon Eustathius and obliged him to confess his perjury and repent.

Three imperial officers were present on the occasion. They went their way, but later, when they themselves were imprisoned and condemned on false charges they remembered the Bishop of Myra, and prayed that through his merits they might be saved. That night Nicholas appeared in a dream to the Emperor Constantine, and to the Prefect and told them to release the men or suffer punishment. The next day emperor and prefect related their dreams to one another. The prisoners were summoned and questioned. When they said that they had asked the intercession of the Bishop of Myra they were released. The emperor sent them to Nicholas with a letter, asking him to withdraw his threats, and pray for the peace of the world.

On another occasion three boys on their way back to school were killed by a local inn-keeper, and their bodies chopped up to be pickled in brine, in order to save on the inn-keeper's butcher's bill. Their families, hearing nothing of their children appealed to Nicholas. He went to the inn, found the brine tubs over which he made the sign of the cross. Out jumped the three lads to be restored to their parents.

Greek historians have claimed (on no perceptible authority) that Nicholas was imprisoned and tortured during the persecution of Diocletian, but released at the accession of Constantine. Also that he was present at the Council of Nicaea. Methodius only commits himself so far as to say that Nicholas preserved his diocese from the Arian heresy at a time when Arianism was rampant in the Eastern Church. Nicholas died about 326.

SHORT VERSION (*St Nicholas*)
Nicholas was Bishop of Myra, a Mediterranean sea-port in the province of Lycia, now in Turkey not far from Rhodes. Little else for certain is known about him apart from the fact that he attended the Council of Nicea in 325. Legends however abound and he is patron Saint of Children, and of Sailors. One story tells of his revival of three boys pickled in brine by an inn-keeper; while another relates how he provided dowries for three girls and thus saved them from the streets. He died soon after Nicaea.

St Ambrose 7 DECEMBER

Bishop of Milan, Teacher of the Faith, 397

St Ambrose was one of the four great Doctors of the Western Church. It was said of him that for fear of God he never feared to speak the truth to kings or any powers. He was born at Trier in the middle of the fourth century, into the family of a prefect of Gaul. His father died while Ambrose was still a child, and his mother returned to Rome with her children.

Ambrose received a good education and was called to the bar, where he practised with such outstanding success that he was made an assessor, and shortly afterwards appointed governor of Liguria and Aemilia by the Emperor Valentinian. During his governorship Ambrose lived in Milan. When he had ruled for two years the see of Milan fell vacant at the death of Bishop Auxentius, an Arian. The election of a new bishop seemed likely to lead to civil disorder, since the city was violently divided between Arians and Catholics. In order to keep the peace, Ambrose attended the church where the election was held and appealed to the people to make their choice peacefully and without demonstrations of ill-feeling. Before he had finished speaking a cry of 'Ambrose for bishop!' was raised by both parties, and to his surprise and dismay the saint found himself proclaimed bishop of Milan.

In an attempt to escape from the undesired distinction thrust upon him Ambrose tried to escape from Milan. He appealed to the emperor, who refused his appeal and remarked only that he was delighted to learn that he had chosen a governor thought fit for episcopal office. After another attempt at escape, Ambrose capitulated.

Although a believer, Ambrose had never been baptised, and this was put right a week before his episcopal consecration, in the year 374. The new bishop now dedicated himself to the service of God; he gave away all he possessed, with the exception of a sum of money for the use of his sister, St Marcellina. He committed the charge of his revenues as bishop to his brother, St Satyrus and, having freed himself from the ties of property, devoted himself to the care of his flock and to the study of theology under St Simplician, a learned Roman priest. Encouraged by St Basil, he abolished all traces of the

Arian heresy in his diocese, except among the Goths, and in a few members of the emperor's household.

Ambrose lived with great austerity. He celebrated the Eucharist for his people daily, and was accessible to them at all times. St Augustine was one of those who thronged to hear him and seek his advice, and it was to St Ambrose that Augustine attributed his final conversion. When he had exhausted every other resource for raising money to redeem captives taken by the Goths in Illyricum and Thrace, he melted down the Church vessels. Accused of sacrilege by the Arians, he replied, 'If the Church possesses gold it is in order to use it for the needy, not to keep it.'

Deeply involved in the complex politics of his day, St Ambrose successfully maintained the spiritual independence of the Church against several emperors. When Empress Justina and her son Valentinian II incited and supported Arian demands, Ambrose stood firm, but without inflaming the Catholics against the Arians. He induced Maximus to confine himself to Gaul, Spain and Britain, when he intended to attack Valentinian II; the first instance of a priest being called upon to use his influence in international politics. When his friend, the Emperor Theodosius, ordered the slaughter of seven thousand in the circus at Thessalonica, Ambrose excommunicated him until Theodosius, in the words of St Ambrose, 'stripped himself of every sign of royalty and bewailed his sin openly in church'.

Although Ambrose did not approve of allowing heretics the free exercise of their religion, he was opposed to bloodshed and, like St Martin, refused to communicate with Ithacius and the other bishops who had procured the execution of Priscillian and his companions. He recommended Christian judges to be as sparing of death sentences as possible: 'When the guilty is slain the criminal is destroyed, but not the crime. But when the criminal is made to turn from the error of his ways, the crime is blotted out and the criminal is saved.' Ambrose died on Good Friday, 4 April 397.

SHORT VERSION (*St Ambrose*)
When Ambrose the Bishop of Milan had exhausted all other means of raising funds to redeem Christian captives taken by

the Goths, he would melt down the church plate. Accused of sacrilege he replied, 'If the Church possesses gold it is in order to use it for the needy, not to keep it.' Such was the measure of the man who never hesitated to tell even Emperors when they were acting wickedly. At the time of his election as Bishop, Ambrose, a trained lawyer, was governor of the city. Passions at the election were rising high and Ambrose forseeing trouble had gone along to beg those assembled to act peaceably. Before he had finished speaking a cry went up, 'Ambrose for bishop' and, despite his protests, he was consecrated in the year 374. He was an enormous influence for good, St Augustine attributed his final conversion to him, and died in Milan on Good Friday, 4 April 397.

St John of the Cross   14 DECEMBER
Mystic, Teacher of the Faith, 1591

In 1567 soon after his ordination to the priesthood John met Teresa of Avila. He was at that time a Carmelite but after Teresa had told him of her plan to restore the primitive Carmelite Rule, he agreed to join her and with two others he did so publicly on 28 November 1568. He became confessor of Teresa's convent of nuns committed to the old rule, but the success of John and Teresa did not gain the approval of the majority of Spanish Carmelites. On 2 December 1577, Carmelites from Toledo seized John and tried to make him renounce his reforms. He refused and so they imprisoned him in a tiny cell where he remained for nine months until he escaped in August in 1578. While in that cell he wrote some of his most famous poems. They are like love poems between the human soul and God. He died at Ubeda in 1591.

St Stephen   26 DECEMBER
The First Martyr

Christian Iconography usually shows St Stephen wearing anachronistically the deacon's dalmatic. It is doubtful, however, if the understanding of the diaconate in the modern Church is the same as that of the Church of the Acts of the Apostles. Stephen was one of seven appointed by the Twelve to deal with the day to day almsgiving and similar good works of the first Christians, having been formally made such by the laying-on of hands. Tradition has it that his martyrdom took place outside the Damascus Gate at Jerusalem, the very gate through which Saul of Tarsus, who looked after the coats of Stephen's executioners, presumably passed as he set out on the journey that would bring him to Christ.

St John the Evangelist

St John the Evangelist, also called the Divine (in the sense of theologian) was a son of Zebedee, and brother to St James, and one of the pair whom our Lord called Boanerges (sons of thunder) perhaps because they wished to command fire from heaven to descend and consume the Samaritan villagers who would not receive him. John was one of the inner circle of apostles, present at the Transfiguration, at the raising of Jairus' daughter, and at Gethsemane during the passion. It was his mother who asked that her two sons might be placed at the right and left hands of the Master when he should come into his kingdom. It was John who asked what should be done with the man who was casting out devils in Christ's name. The brothers seem to have been full of zeal, but inclined to severity.

It was to John that Christ commended his mother, when the disciple stood at the foot of the cross with Mary and the other woman. When the news of the Resurrection was brought to him he ran to the tomb with St Peter, reached the tomb first, but waited for Peter to enter, 'and he saw and believed'. He was one of the seven disciples who went fishing on the Sea of Tiberias, and was the first to recognise Jesus standing on the shore, and said to Peter, 'It is the Lord.'

In the Acts, John was with Peter when the lame man was healed at the Beautiful Gate of the Temple, and went down to Samaria with him to lay hands on those that had been baptised. When St Paul went up to Jerusalem after his conversion he was interrogated by James, Peter and John, and John was present at the Council of Jerusalem.

It is uncertain when he left Jerusalem, probably after the martyrdom of Peter and Paul. He settled at Ephesus, but there is a tradition that he visited Rome and was thrown into a bath of boiling oil outside the Latin Gate, from which he miraculously escaped uninjured. This is the origin of the feast on 6 May of St John before the Latin Gate.

According to Eusebius he was condemned to exile in the island of Patmos during the persecution of Domitian, and there saw the Revelation. After the death of Domitian, John was free to return to Ephesus, and he governed the churches of Asia from that city.

Once on a visit to a neighbouring city in Asia Minor, he confided to a new bishop the care of a promising youth. The young man was baptised, but afterwards lapsed, fell into evil ways and became captain of a band of robbers. When John revisited the place he asked the bishop for 'the deposit which I and Christ committed to you. I demand the young man, and the soul of a brother.' The bishop groaned and said: 'He is dead, dead to God.' John replied: 'I left a fine keeper of a brother's soul; but get me a horse and a guide.' He had himself guided to the district where the robbers operated, and was taken prisoner. He demanded to be taken to the captain, and when the young man recognised him he tried to get away. John followed and cried after him: 'Why do you flee, my son, from me your father, your defenceless aged father?' And he would not let him go until he brought him back repentant.

At Ephesus he is said to have opposed the heretic Cerinthus, and once, on entering the baths with his disciple Polycarp, he learned that Cerinthus was within. He turned back, saying, 'Let us make haste and be gone, lest the bath wherein is Cerinthus, the enemy of truth, should fall upon our heads.' In his old age he is said to have amused himself with a tame partridge, and when blamed for such frivolity, to have said, 'The bow cannot always be bent.'

Jerome describes how, when so old that he had to be carried into church, his sermons always consisted of the words, 'Little children, love one another.' When asked why he always repeated these words, he replied, 'Because it is the word of the Lord, and if you keep it you do enough.'

St John died at Ephesus about the third year of Trajan. He was probably about ninety-four, the only one of the Apostles known positively not to have been martyred.

SHORT VERSION (*St John the Evangelist*)
John, together with his brother James, was a follower of Jesus from almost the beginning. He was one of the inner circle of apostles and, with his brother and Peter, he was a witness to the raising of Jairus' daughter, and the Transfiguration, and he was close to Jesus in Gethsemane on the night of his arrest. It was to

John that Christ commended his mother; John was the only one of the Twelve to stand at the foot of the cross. And according to the Gospels it was John who ran with Peter to the empty tomb and when he saw believed. Tradition has it that he left Jerusalem only after the martyrdom of Peter and Paul, and settled in Ephesus, but during the Domitian persecutions was exiled to the island of Patmos where he wrote his Revelation. After Domitian's death John is said to have returned to Ephesus where he died at the age of ninety-four.

St Thomas Becket 29 DECEMBER
Archbishop of Canterbury, Martyr, 1170

Thomas Becket was the son of a prosperous Norman sheriff of London. His life was characterised by violent contrasts of fortune; educated by the canons of Merton, in Surrey, he emerged from a privileged childhood to experience virtual poverty. By the time he was twenty-one he had lost both his parents and was obliged to work for a living in the commercial offices in London. Soon his gift for administration and his personal qualities had gained for him a privileged position with the burghers of London. To one in particular, Richer de l'Aigle, whom he often accompanied in field sports, he owed his lifelong love of hawking and hunting, at which he excelled.

The turning point in Thomas's career came when he was no more than twenty-four. He was appointed to the household of Theobald, Archbishop of Canterbury, where his energy, intelligence and charm earned him rapid promotion. The archbishop conferred on him several benefices, and within twelve years he was ordained deacon, and nominated Archdeacon of Canterbury. He was described as 'blithe of countenance . . . winning and lovable in his conversation, frank of speech, but slightly stuttering in his talk, so keen of discernment and understanding that he could always make difficult questions plain after a wise manner'.

King Henry II was not slow to appreciate the quality of this young officer of the Church, whose tastes and skill in the hunting field, and whose directness in attaining his objectives, matched his own. Soon, he added gratitude to his initial liking for Thomas, for it was by the archdeacon's intervention in Rome that Pope Eugenius III ruled against Stephen's son Eustace as a successor to the throne of England. Henry's title was then secure.

The bond of friendship between the king and the churchman, prefiguring in its warmth and tempestuousness the tragic association of Henry VIII and Thomas More, quickly elevated Thomas to one of the highest offices in the kingdom. At thirty-six, 'Thomas of London', as he had been known not long since, was appointed Chancellor. Thus he entered the lists in which the claims of his conscience (which would not admit of compromise) would often be pitted against the ambitions of a king determined to impose his will in all things throughout his realm in England and France. Totally committed to the king's interests, Thomas made good use of Henry's confidence to prevail upon him to moderate some of the more savage laws to which his people were subject.

As yet, however, the disparity of principles, if not entirely of character, had not been manifested. 'The king and chancellor', went the popular saying, 'have but one heart and one mind'. At this stage Thomas belonged as much in the world as did the king, who was far from resenting the magnificence with which his chancellor surrounded himself. When Thomas went as Henry's ambassador, the splendour of his entourage and the richness of his gifts dazzled his hosts. 'If this be but the chancellor, what must his king's state be?' they asked. In support of his master's war in France, Thomas led his own men to Toulouse. He rode at the head of seven hundred of his knights, and personally led the assaults, clad in armour. The Prior of Leicester, meeting Thomas in Rouen, reproached him with looking more like a falconer than a cleric. Thomas, good-humouredly, admitted the justice of this remark, but in spite of his worldliness, and the new magnificence, he never broke faith with an allegiance of greater importance than the temporal. He made regular retreats at Merton, and there gladly accepted all the rigours of monastic discipline. His confessor, Robert, Prior of Merton, who was at his side throughout his life and at the hour of his death, attested that in his private life Thomas never capitulated to the manifold temptations which beset the paths of the great.

When, in 1161, Archbishop Theobald died, scarcely anyone questioned the suitability of Thomas as his successor. The archdeacon himself foresaw the conflict into which his conscience would drive him in his dealings with the king. His clear-sightedness was never more apparent than when he told Henry: 'Should God permit me to be Archbishop of Canterbury I should soon lose your Majesty's favour, and the affection with which you honour me would be changed into hatred.' Henry would take no refusal, and any remonstrance from Thomas was over-ruled by the Papal Legate. He was ordained priest on the Saturday in Whitsun week, 1162, and consecrated bishop the next day.

In opposition to the wishes of the king, the new archbishop relinquished the office of Chancellor, and with it all the trappings of secular authority. Under his cassock he wore a hair shirt. He dined abstemiously among learned men, his monks and regulars. The reading aloud from a good book was substituted for conversation. Laymen were entertained suitably at a more bountiful table. Thomas observed a strict rule of life, 'His hours of sleep were short because of his service to the poor, his tears and penance, his prayers and studies.' He had always been liberal to the poor. Now he showed special care for the unfortunate, not only in almsgiving, but in visiting and in vigilant concern for their welfare. 'He was meek towards those of little might, but mighty and zealous towards the ribald.' To the end of his days he was by nature proud, impetuous and hot-tempered, but his attendant clergy were enjoined to speak their minds whenever they found him at fault. 'For four eyes see more clearly than two,' he told them.

In one thing only Thomas was resolved to defer to no authority other than that of the Church; the defence of this Church and its rights, which were not to be subordinated to the temporal aims of the State. Few English clergy at that time would have had the courage to embrace such a policy. From the placing in opposite camps of two such inflexible minds, each assured of the justice of his aims, proceeded the mounting enmity between king and archbishop which Thomas had foretold.

Occasions for conflict between the Church and the court quickly multiplied, as the archbishop made it plain to the king that he would never surrender the integrity of the Church. In particular he was resolved that the Church, and those who served it, should be ruled by ecclesiastical law, and not by the barbarous, and far from impartial, civil courts. Less than a century had elapsed since the Conquest, and blinding and maiming were familiar punishments meted on the smallest evidence of insurrection.

So began a war of attrition. As the archbishop strove to accommodate himself to the king's will, so much more exacting did the royal demands become. Thomas persevered until, at the Council of Clarendon, near Salisbury, it became plain that the king would be content with nothing less than the complete surrender of the Church's right to appeal to the pope. A number of bishops aligned themselves on the side of the lords and the king.

At this crisis, Thomas arraigned, not those who deserted, but himself for the concessions he had been prepared to make. His self-reproach was shown in his own words: 'I am a proud, vain man, a feeder of birds and a follower of hounds and I have been made a shepherd of sheep. I am fit only to be cast out of the See I fill.' In repentance for having wavered, he imposed penance on himself in which he continued until he was absolved by the pope.

He now turned to the source of his spiritual authority, to Rome, only to find himself a prisoner. He made two attempts to embark, and on each occasion was turned back at the coast. Then came the command to wait upon the king in council at Northampton. So stormy was the meeting that it was clear that no reconciliation was possible.

In October of the same year, Thomas succeeded in escaping, and set sail for France. At Sens he met Pope Alexander III and submitted to him the sixteen Constitutions of Clarendon which the king's party were determined to enforce and the pope rebuked him for having temporised as far as he had. Thomas removed his ring of the See of Canterbury and placed it in the pope's hands, confessing himself unworthy of his office. The pope, reinstating him, told him that to abandon his trust would be to abandon the cause of God.

The king now turned upon those who had supported the archbishop, confiscated all they had, and told them to join their insubordinate priest in exile. The pope had offered Thomas the hospitality of the Cistercian monastery at Potigny, to which he withdrew to enjoy greater peace than he had known for years, as an unprivileged member of the community. Henry, still unappeased, told the general chapter of the Cistercians that if they continued to harbour the rebel he would sequestrate all their possessions in his dominion. St Thomas left Potigny and entered the abbey of St Columba as the guest of King Louis VII of France.

During the six years which Thomas spent in France, he

regarded his exile as a spiritual retreat, and an occasion for the expiation of his sins. After many fruitless embassies between England and France, Henry himself came to parley with his archbishop in the presence of the pope and the French king, but the deadlock was not resolved.

In July, 1170, King Henry and his archbishop met in Normandy, and against all expectations, and with no evidence of willingness to retract, on either side, they agreed to bury the past. To Thomas, the call once again to become 'a shepherd of sheep' was decisive, but he had no illusions. As he bade farewell to the Bishop of Paris, he said: 'I am going to England to die.' To the common people of Kent, who came in their multitudes to welcome their archbishop, it seemed a triumph, and the return of peace. 'Blessed is he who comes in the name of the Lord!' they called, and Thomas had a better homecoming than he had ever known in the years of his splendour.

To the intransigent bishops, whose denial of the Church's cause Thomas had never condoned, the renewed authority of Canterbury boded no good. Assiduously they laid their complaints about the archbishop before the king, and it is unlikely that they failed to recall the moral victory which the priest had won. Thomas refused to lift from them the ban of excommunication, and it is not hard to visualise the circumstances in which Henry, at Bur, uttered the words which some of his hearers took as a mandate for the assassination of Thomas Becket. Four knights; Reginald Fitzurse, William de Tracy, Hugh de Morville and Richard le Breton, set off from Bur, emboldened by the belief that they bore the king's authority. On 29 December 1170, they confronted Thomas with many of the old demands, and in particular that he should exculpate three bishops who continued under his censure. The archbishop gave them the answer which he had given so often before to the king.

Fully armed, the knights returned to the cathedral as vespers were being sung, terrifying the monks, who closed the door of the North Transept against them. It was Thomas himself who cried, 'Away, you cowards!' and swung back the door to give them entry. While all the chapter fled to the sanctuary of the crypt, Thomas stood fast, companioned only by three, one of whom was his confessor, Robert, prior of Merton. The knights tried to drag the archbishop from the sacred precincts. Thomas cried, 'I am ready to die, but God's curse be on you if you harm my people.' William de Tracy struck with his sword, and although Edward Grim, an English monk, deflected the blow with his arm, the steel wounded the archbishop's head, so that the blood ran into his eyes. Thomas knew that his life was ended, 'Into your hands, O Lord, I commend my spirit', he cried, and as de Tracy struck again, flinging him to his knees, he was heard to say, 'For the name of Jesus and in defence of the Church I am willing to die.' With a great blow, le Breton severed the top of the Archbishop's head. The thunder which, it is recorded, crashed over the cathedral as the murderers retreated, seemed to have its reverberations throughout Europe. Even in an age habituated to violence and political murder, the martyrdom of Thomas of Canterbury struck horror, and he was canonised in July 1174.

SHORT VERSION (*St Thomas Becket*)

'Who will rid me of this pestilent priest?' fumed England's King Henry II. The 'priest' was his Archbishop of Canterbury, appointed by himself eight years previously. He had hoped to control the Church by his appointment because, up to then, Thomas had been his Chancellor and his friend. His scheme had not worked. Thomas had been faithful to his new charge and within a year of his consecration, king and archbishop were at loggerheads. That quarrel lasted seven years with Thomas in exile in France. He returned to Canterbury in the summer of 1170, but within months trouble brewed again as Thomas asserted the rights of the Church against those of the king. Four knights overheard the King's remark about Thomas. Swiftly they took horse for Canterbury and slew the Archbishop in his Cathedral on 29 December 1170.

Josephine Butler
Social Reformer, Wife, Mother, 1907

It seems hard to believe that the British Government in the last century actually set up brothels in garrison towns in England. The scheme raised little objection in Parliament, but Josephine Butler, whose husband was at the time Principal of Liverpool College, took up the cause of homeless young women who so easily were forced to earn a living by selling their bodies. She launched her campaign in 1869, and then began years of enormous activity, in which she travelled throughout the land, often at considerable risk to herself (for there was much opposition) addressing meetings, organising petitions and generally co-ordinating the efforts of those who wanted to see the Acts abolished. It took at least fourteen years to achieve their end. For the rest of her days, Josephine remained a great power for good in England, until she died in her birthplace, to which she had retired, in 1906.

John Wyclif

31 DECEMBER

Theologian, Reformer, 1384

John Wyclif was an Oxford scholar, born a Yorkshireman, probably near Richmond. He was successively Master of Balliol and Warden of Canterbury College and in 1366 attracted public notice when he published a controversial tract about the taxation of the clergy by Parliament, and the payment of tribute exacted by the Pope at the time of King John. John Wycliff generally disapproved of the papal action and slowly his views hardened over the last fifteen years of his life, leading him to dispute the authority of Rome, as it was then exercised. He was employed by Edward III in 1374 as an ambassador to papal delegates, over a question of appointments to benefices, while in 1372 he became Vicar of Lutterworth which post he retained until his death. In the Spring of 1378 he was tried for heresy. Wycliff had constantly attacked the worldliness of many of the monks and friars, and for that matter of the Pope himself, and he claimed that even the Pope was not immune from accusation even by a layman if he had done wrong. John Wyclif had too powerful a group of friends and patrons to be found guilty, but when he left Lambeth, where his trial had taken place, he began to gather a group of preachers around him to go up and down the land preaching the Gospel free of all the common superstitious additions. At the same time he began to translate the Bible into English. He did not do all the work himself, and each copy had to be written out by hand exactly as the monks used to make copies of the Vulgate. In 1382 he was tried a second time for heresy. Although he was forced to leave Oxford he was never formally excommunicated, and so he died in his parish in 1384.

Index